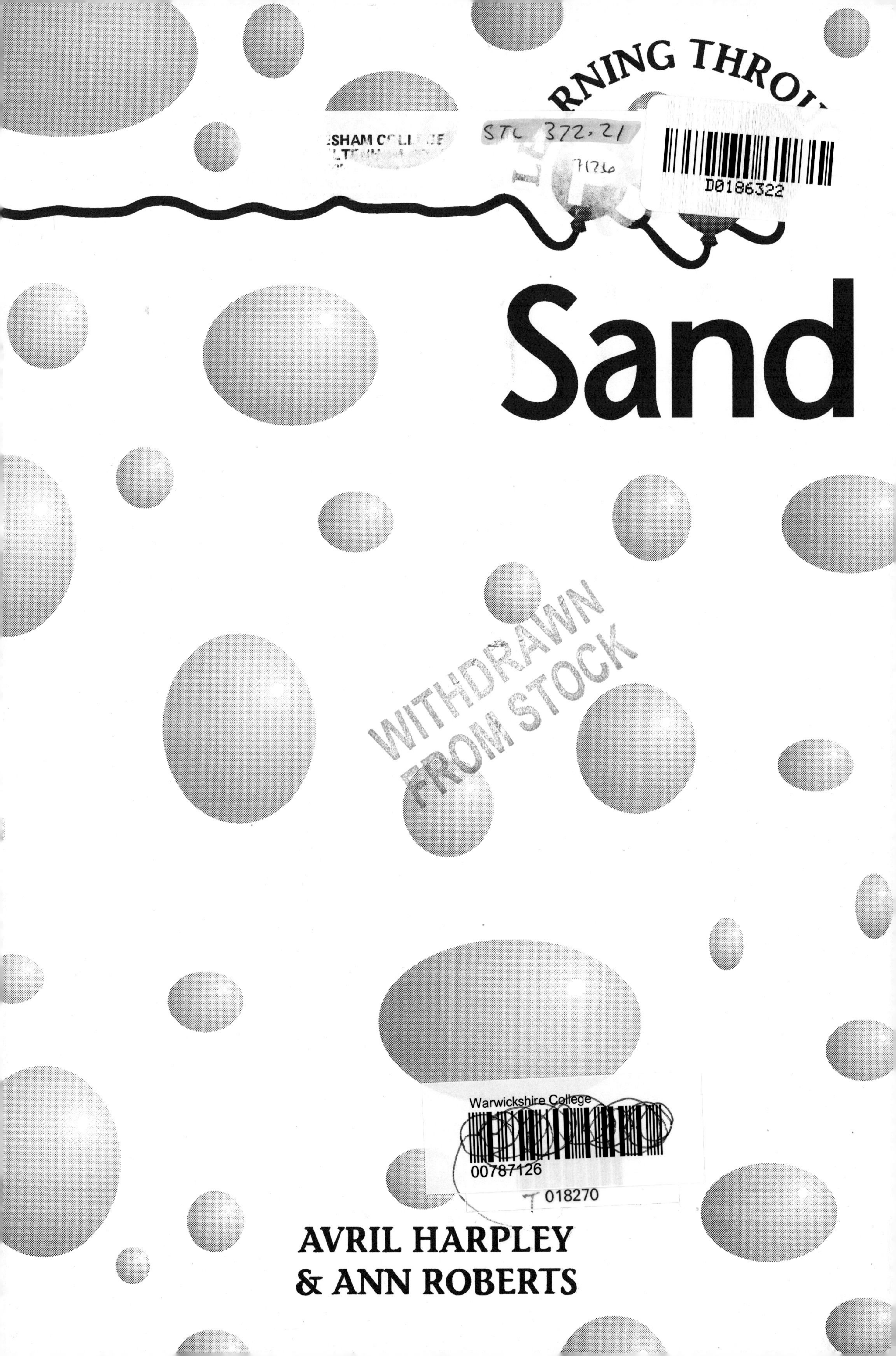

LEARNING THROUGH

Sand

AVRIL HARPLEY
& ANN ROBERTS

Published by Scholastic Ltd,
Villiers House,
Clarendon Avenue,
Leamington Spa,
Warwickshire CV32 5PR

4 5 6 7 8 9 0   8 9 0 1 2 3 4 5

Authors
Avril Harpley and Ann Roberts

Editor
Jane Bishop

Assistant Editor
Sally Gray

Series designer
Lynne Joesbury

Designers
Anna Oliwa and Lynda Murray

Illustrations
Claire Boyce

Cover photograph
Fiona Pragoff

Designed using Aldus Pagemaker

British Library Cataloguing-in-Publication Data
A catalogue record for this book is available from the British Library.

ISBN 0-590-53636-2

CONTENTS

INTRODUCTION 5

CHAPTER ONE: LANGUAGE AND LITERACY

- WRITE ON 11
- JACK AND THE BEANSTALK 12
- OLD MACDONALD 13
- TEDDY AT THE SEASIDE 14
- MAGIC JEWELS 15
- SAND JOURNEY 16
- RHYMING GAMES 17
- SAND POEM 18

CHAPTER TWO: MATHEMATICS

- IMPRESSIONS 19
- FILL THAT SHAPE 20
- SAFARI WORLD 21
- DINOSAUR WORLD 22
- MAKE THAT PATTERN 23
- FIVE CURRANT BUNS 24
- MOVE IT! 25
- MAKE THAT NUMBER 26

CHAPTER THREE: PERSONAL AND SOCIAL DEVELOPMENT

- TAKE CARE TURTLES 27
- UNDERGROUND OVERGROUND 28
- HOUSES 29
- PIZZA GALORE! 30
- SAND PATTERNS 31
- CHICKEN AND EGG 32
- THE GOOD SAMARITAN 33
- STEP THE STONES 34

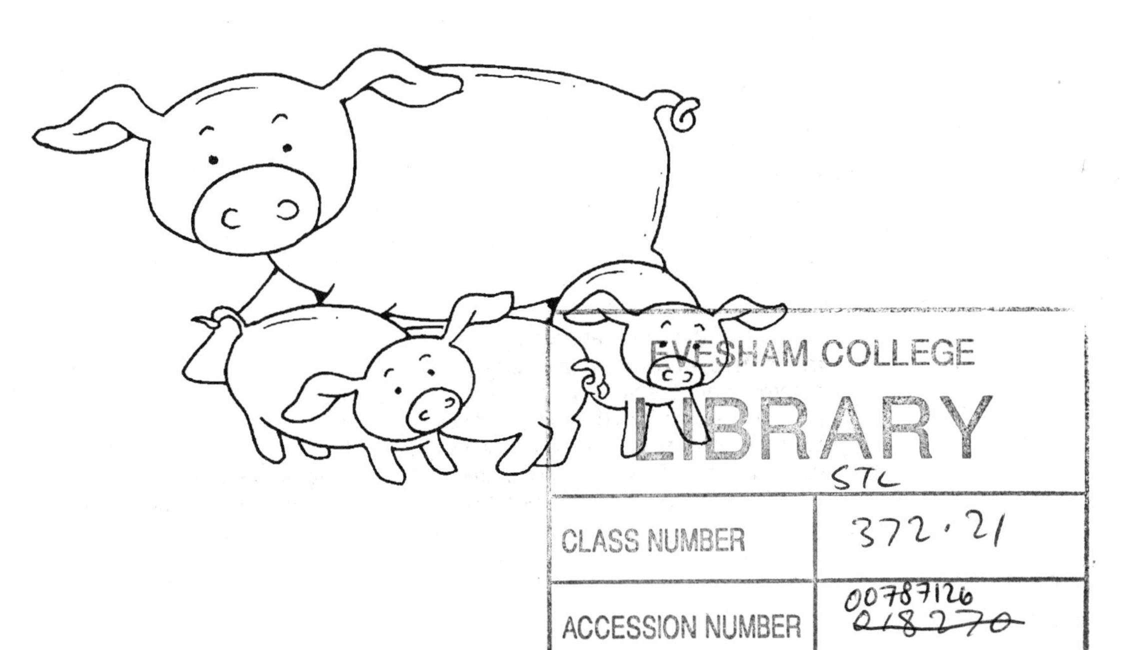

CHAPTER FOUR: KNOWLEDGE AND UNDERSTANDING OF THE WORLD

THE BUILDING SITE 35
GARDENING FUN! 36
ROCK AND ROLL 37
SNAKES AND STONES 38
PIRATE'S TREASURE 39
INSECT WORLD 40
NEIGHBOURHOOD WATCH 41
BIRTHDAY TEA 42

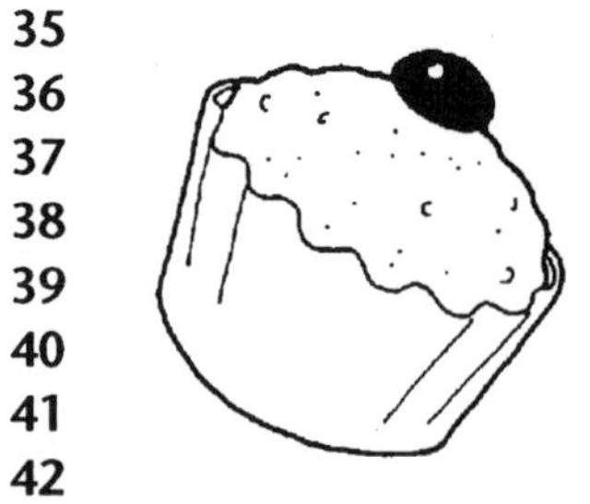

CHAPTER FIVE: PHYSICAL DEVELOPMENT

ROLL THE CONKER 43
SANDPIES 44
MASHER 45
TRICKLE TREAT 46
FEEL IT 47
DIG IT 48
HIT AND MISS 49
DIG DEEP 50

CHAPTER SIX: CREATIVE DEVELOPMENT

SAND SCULPTURES 51
STICKPICS 52
MIX AND MOULD 53
DENS 54
THE PICNIC DANCE 55
COMB IT! 56
SAND MUSIC 57
SAND PAINTING 58

PHOTOCOPIABLES

TEDDY AT THE SEASIDE 59
SAND JOURNEY 60
DINOSAUR WORLD 61
THE BUILDING SITE 62
GARDENING FUN! 63
MIX AND MOULD 64

INTRODUCTION

Sand is one of the world's natural resources. People of all ages are attracted to sand and young children in particular find it an exciting and satisfying material with which to work and play.

Sand is a sensory material that has tactile and therapeutic properties. It is easy to handle and encourages success, children cannot fail with sand. Working with sand provides one of the first hand experiences that are an essential part of early years learning, allowing children to explore and investigate for themselves.

Learning through play

Sand play provides a wealth of educational opportunities. With a combination of free and structured play it is possible to develop the children's skills across the six Areas of Learning, as recommended by SCAA as desirable outcomes for children's learning.

Most adults that work closely with young children agree that children need an element of freedom to work individually to explore and investigate materials such as sand through their play. They need to experience the sense of wonderment and excitement that lies embedded in early childhood.

Once the children have had plenty of experience of free play with sand, their learning can be extended by providing a well-structured programme of activities, utilising a greater range of resources.

Resources should be changed frequently to provide new challenges and experiences. They should at times be natural, such as shells, stones and fir cones and at other times include 'small world' toys, such as zoo and farm animals, Playmobil and LEGO. Let your imagination run free and explore all the resources that you have in your learning environment (ensuring that they are safe for children to handle).

The resources need to be planned carefully, selected and displayed in a stimulating way. Following this, the children will need to be given plenty of time and encouragement to explore, ask questions and investigate.

Setting up

Children need to experience more than one variety of sand. There are many types available, such as, builders' sand, which is soft; red or sharp sand and silver sand, which is fine, and used a lot in nurseries and schools. In addition to the varieties of sand, by making sand wet or damp you can create a variety of different effects or textures for the children to explore.

Having selected the type of sand you will use, choose the container and location for the sand. If you do not have sufficient space for a sand trolley or sand pit, it is possible to use small table-top trays, though these will obviously contain less sand and will restrict the play to one or two children at a time. Using sand outside works well (and there is, of course, less concern about mess). If using sand inside, position the sand trolley in an area of the room that is safe and away from the carpeted area. Whether you are using sand inside or outside, you will need a dustpan and brush/broom close at hand. If possible, include some child-sized equipment amongst your resources to involve children in the responsibility of tidying-up.

Planning and preparation

Sand activities need to be planned well in advance, ensuring that the sand is prepared and the necessary resources collected.

Consider how you will introduce the activity to the children; what will you say, do and ask? Think about what you will provide for the children if they finish much more quickly than you anticipated. Don't forget to plan the location of the sand tray based on safety and access, flooring and space.

The role of the adult

The adult's role is one of 'constructive intervention', being aware of what the children are doing and extending their understanding. There is a fine line between this and 'destructive intervention', that of taking over the activity to such an extent that the child withdraws and loses the desire to find out for him/herself.

Intervention is a skill which comes with good observation skills and an understanding of child development. You must be prepared to vary your role according to the situation. Sometimes it is necessary to act as a passive observer or interested listener and at other times you will need to lead the child on to investigate further by using open-ended questions such as: What do you think will happen next?; What happened when you tried it out?

Adults who explore the educational possibilities of sand play with their children, will find that it is as demanding and stimulating as any other area of early years learning.

Resources and storage

Collect your sand and resources for sand play from a variety of sources: educational catalogues, toy shops, garden centres and reclaimed materials from around the home. If using reclaimed or improvised materials check that the material they are made from is safe and has been thoroughly cleaned, as many children have allergies to certain products and young children in general are likely to put things in their mouths!

Try and include a variety of shapes, sizes and colours, such as yoghurt pots, margarine tubs and detergent bottles, also include some transparent bottles such as fruit squash and shampoo bottles. Holes can be made in them, making them useful for investigations and experiments.

Sand itself must be washed regularly and changed. It should be covered when not in use to prevent unwelcome visitors, to extend its life and to prevent it from being spread around the room/area. To cover a sand pit you may either use a commercial covering or a large piece of plastic sheeting (CARE! Do not allow the children to play with these). A piece of wood or a drape may be adequate to cover a sand tray. Store sand in the plastic bag in which it was bought, with the top twisted or tied.

As you build up your resources for sand play, it is essential that you store them carefully and in an accessible manner, cleaning, disinfecting and drying them regularly, so that they are always ready to use when you need them. It is a good idea to store the equipment in labelled sets, such as; 'pouring and filling', 'moulds and prints' (containing sets of basic equipment) and in other categories such as 'Crocodile world'. You may choose to put the equipment in plastic wallets and inside sturdy storage containers. Don't forget to check the items regularly to ensure that all the items have been put back and not lost or mislaid.

Organisation

There is a good deal of flexibility when working with sand; group size can vary between individuals, pairs and small groups, and it can be used indoors or outside.

Don't overcrowd the sand tray, children need the space to be able to reach into the tray with enough elbow room to allow them to manipulate the resources as well as their own bodies.

Providing sufficient resources and a good variety of activities is a fundamental consideration in order to achieve the best learning potential from sand play.

All children need to be aware of the need not to throw sand or ignore it if it falls on the floor.

Observation and assessment

Because of the small numbers of children involved, at any one time, with a sand activity it provides a good opportunity for you to observe and assess their progress.

To make the most of any observation it is necessary to be well prepared. By keeping a small notebook or file with simple grids drawn onto the pages, you stand more chance of remembering your observations in detail, such as the vocabulary used by the child. Include in your notes information such as context, time, group size, activity and recommended action or follow-up.

Restrict observations to bursts of two to five minutes to allow the activity to be sustained and for the child to receive the necessary adult intervention and input.

Decide on the focus of your observation in advance, for example, does the child have an understanding of a concept, can they master a certain skill, or has their vocabulary in this area developed?

In order to get an accurate picture of a child's understanding you will need to vary the techniques used in your assessment. Try to ensure that in addition to observing the children and listening to their language and vocabulary, you employ questioning and problem-solving skills. The results of your assessments should be used to inform and aid your planning.

Progress in learning can occur at very different rates across a group of young children and so assessment may need to be more frequent with some children than others. Children with special needs will require a sensitive and realistic approach and observation is a very supportive tool to them.

Links with home

If you have captured a child's interest in the activities presented to them, they may retell or imitate the activity in their home setting. Try sending home a newsletter, including photographs to show parents what the children are doing. This will help parents to understand what learning experiences their children are having.

Make some simple packs with activity instructions for parents to borrow. This will encourage liaison between parents and your setting and the children will benefit by using similar equipment and play at home. Encourage the parents to make observations, which they can relate to you after they have tried an activity at home. This additional information is a valuable assessment tool.

Story books relating to sand such as *Bears' Seaside Adventure*, Prue Theobalds (Uplands Books) are a valuable resource. Have some ready for the parents to borrow and share with their children at home. This will provide an additional opportunity for the children to relate their learning experiences.

Health and safety

Working with young children and sand raises a number of health and safety issues, that the adult helpers need to be constantly aware of. In order to draw the readers' attention to this area within the text a CARE! warning is included in this book to highlight potential hazards.

One of the first things that you need to do is to clearly explain to the children that they must not throw sand and must always get help to clear up the sand if they spill it on the floor. Children will need reminding of the dangers on a regular basis, as they tend to forget, especially when they are engrossed in an activity! If a child does get some sand in their eyes, try to keep the child calm and ensure that they do not rub their eyes, seek medical attention from a first-aider/school nurse as soon as possible.

Slipping on the floor where sand has been spilt is a common accident. Try to avoid this by encouraging the children to be as vigilant as you are in keeping the floor regularly swept, and as soon as a spillage occurs. Don't forget to allocate sufficient time for tidying-up, making sure that the children are involved in this process as much as possible and telling them how helpful they have been!

How to use this book

The chapters in this book are organised into the six Areas of Learning for the under-fives that have been identified by the School Curriculum and Assessment Authority. These areas are Language and Literacy (Chapter 1), Mathematics (Chapter 2), Personal and Social Development (Chapter 3), Knowledge and Understanding of the World (Chapter 4), Physical Development (Chapter 5) and Creative Development (Chapter 6). The activities in this book are directly linked to these areas.

The activities are practical, may be used in a variety of settings and are planned to stimulate and develop young children's experience of sand. Each activity has a key learning objective.

For each activity, advice is given regarding the size of the group, how to set up the activity, the resources that are needed and step-by-step instructions of how to perform the activity with the children. In addition there are ideas for adaptations of the main activity with respect to meeting the needs of older and younger children and ideas for follow-up activities showing cross-curricular links. Suggestions for questions to ask relating to each activity are included.

Included in the book there is a section with six photocopiable activity sheets; each page cross-referenced and related to a specific activity detailed earlier in the book. Finally, the following page contains a photocopiable 'topic web' which shows all the activities in the book with their page references.

SAND

LANGUAGE AND LITERACY

Write on, page 11
Jack and the beanstalk, page 12
Old MacDonald, page 13
Teddy at the seaside, page 14
Magic jewels, page 15
Sand journey, page 16
Rhyming games, page 17
Sand poem, page 18

KNOWLEDGE AND UNDERSTANDING OF THE WORLD

The building site, page 35
Gardening fun!, page 36
Rock and roll, page 37
Snakes and stones, page 38
Pirate's treasure, page 39
Insect world, page 40
Neighbourhood watch, page 41
Birthday tea, page 42

PHYSICAL DEVELOPMENT

Roll the conker, page 43
Sandpies, page 44
Masher, page 45
Trickle treat, page 46
Feel it, page 47
Dig it, page 48
Hit and miss, page 49
Dig deep, page 50

MATHEMATICS

Impressions, page 19
Fill that shape, page 20
Safari world, page 21
Dinosaur world, page 22
Make that pattern, page 23
Five currant buns, page 24
Move it!, page 25
Make that number, page 26

PERSONAL AND SOCIAL DEVELOPMENT

Take care turtles, page 27
Underground overground, page 28
Houses, page 29
Pizza galore!, page 30
Sand patterns, page 31
Chicken and egg, page 32
The good Samaritan, page 33
Step the stones, page 34

CREATIVE DEVELOPMENT

Sand sculptures, page 51
Stickpics, page 52
Mix and mould, page 53
Dens, page 54
The picnic dance, page 55
Comb it!, page 56
Sand music, page 57
Sand painting, page 58

These activities provide ideas showing how the use of sand can help develop children's language and literacy skills. Some of the activities encourage the skills of speaking and listening, whilst others use story, rhyme or song as a stimulus.

WRITE ON

Learning objective
To develop hand control and to explore and experiment with mark-making to communicate meaning.

Group size
Individual, or a group of up to six children.

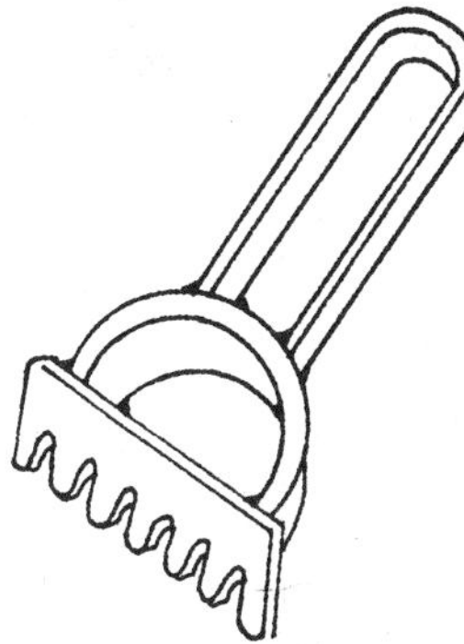

What you need
The sand tray and individual shallow trays, baking trays or palettes. Mark-making objects, (forks, sticks, pencils, combs and rakes), silver sand, water, dustpan and brush.

Setting up
Fill the tray with the fine sand and gather the mark-making objects together, ready for use.

What to do
To begin with, allow the children some freedom to play with the sand, using just their hands. They will enjoy the sensations of sand trickling through their fingers, scooping and digging.

Introduce the idea of making marks, beginning with one of the instruments. Show them how to make marks going in one direction, then up, down, sideways. Ask them to try, showing them ways of varying the action to slow, fast, stroking, scrubbing and so on. Challenge them to make lines, wiggles, waves and loops. Observe the children closely, noting their ability to control the direction of their marks and their ability to copy or follow your instructions.

After a while, dampen the sand. They will be able to make deeper impressions in the damp sand. Let them finish by experimenting.

Questions to ask
What does it feel like? Can you make a mark, a line, a squiggle in the sand? Can you copy my marks? What else can you do?

For younger children
Younger children will need plenty of opportunities such as this, in order to develop the fine muscle control needed before they can grasp and control a pencil. Allow them to try a variety of tools and help them to practise simple lines and loops.

For older children
Observe them closely, looking for any signs that demonstrate the beginnings of writing: moving from left to right, making loops and recognising shapes. Help them to recognise some letter shapes that you draw in the sand for them. Are they able to draw any from their own name?

Follow-up activities
- Create a well-resourced writing area.
- Create a role-play area where writing is an integral part of the play, such as an office.
- Use fingers to make letters in messy materials, such as, shaving foam and chocolate sauce.

JACK AND THE BEANSTALK

Learning objective
To listen and respond to a traditional story. To retell a story in their own words.

Group size
Whole group.

What you need
Sand tray, individual trays, Play people, twigs, small world house, story of *Jack and the Beanstalk* (Ladybird).

Setting up
Ask the children to help you set up the scene of Jack's house in the sand tray. Use the twigs to represent the beanstalk.

What to do
Tell the story to the whole group. Show them how you use the props in the sand tray to tell the story to them. Encourage the children to join in with the repetitive phrases. You may signal to them to say 'Fee-Fi-Fo-Fum...', by holding up a pretend giant to stimulate their memory. Encourage the children to use different voices for Jack, his mother and the giant.

The children can then work in pairs to retell their favourite part of the story in small sand trays, using some of their own chosen props to help them.

Questions to ask
Ask questions about the story to check the children's understanding: How did Jack's mother feel when he sold the cow? How did Jack get to the castle? Can they think of another way of ending the story?

For younger children
Concentrate on one aspect of the story with the children. Help them to use the props in the sand to develop their comparative vocabulary. For example, ask them to describe where Jack is, as you move him around the sand tray. He could be going up the beanstalk or coming down, going into the house or out of the castle. Can they give you instructions of where to place him?

For older children
Can the children sequence the story. As you tell them the story ask them what they think might happen next. Allow the children to predict and discuss their ideas.

Make a large zigzag book with the children showing the main sequence of events in the story. You could write down their ideas as you create the book together.

Follow-up activities
- Plant some bean sprouts.
- Use the idea of 'giant' and 'small' in movement. Ask the children to move with small/giant movements.
- Make a display of objects in small and giant sizes with corresponding labels.

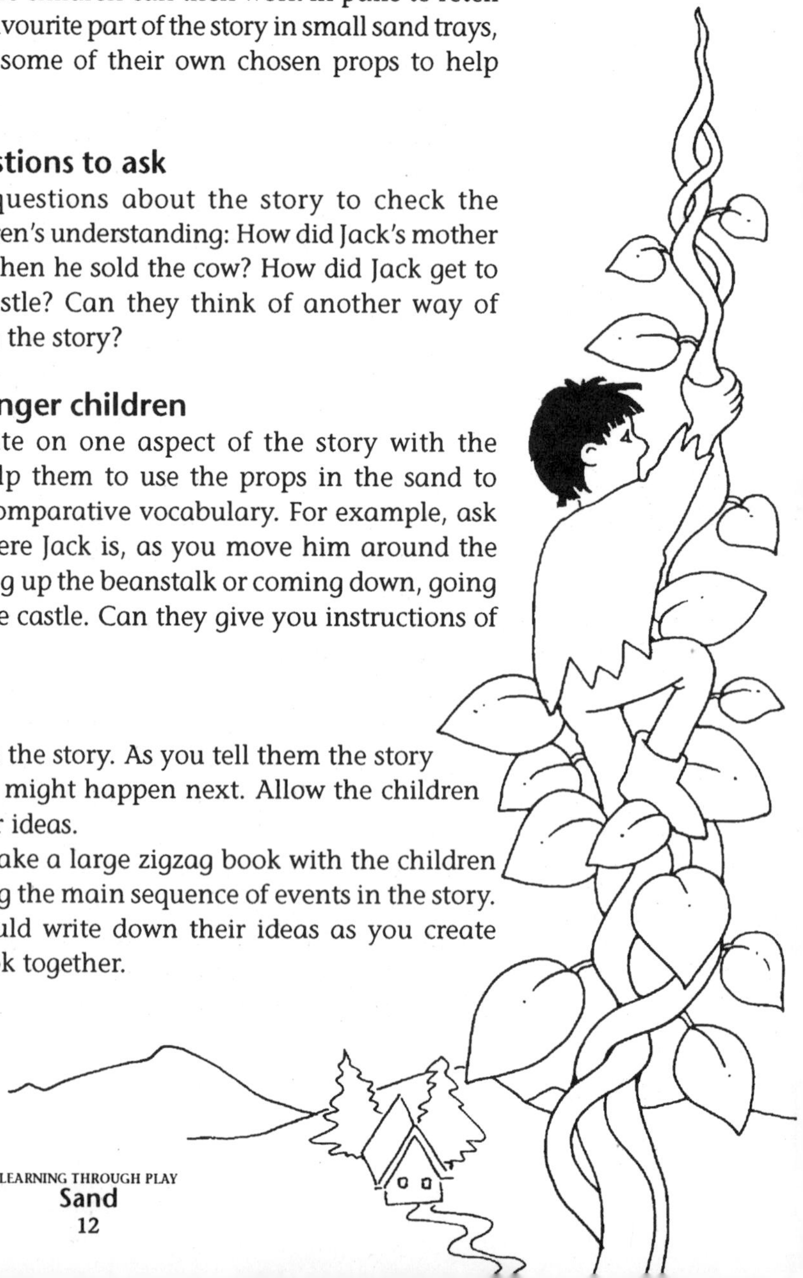

OLD MACDONALD

Learning objective
To encourage children to listen attentively and to develop skills of sequencing stories and songs.

Group size
Whole group and smaller group work.

What you need

Words for 'Old Macdonald had a farm', a collection of farm animals and buildings, the sand tray, (you could use compost instead of sand for a more realistic feel and smell).

Setting up

Let the children help you set up the farm, deciding where the animals will go, the position of the farmhouse and buildings.

What to do

Sing the song with the children, encouraging them to make the appropriate animal noises at the right time. Explain that the sand tray is going to be Macdonald's farm.

Make up a story about the farmer and his animals. As you tell the story move the animals around the tray and encourage the children to join in with the animal sounds as you mention the animal names. Ask the children for their ideas for the next thing the farmer could do. Allow the child who has each idea to move the farmer along to his next job.

In pairs or small groups allow the children some free play with the resources, encouraging them to tell simple stories to each other. Observe and intervene when appropriate, helping the children to sequence their thoughts and develop their vocabulary.

Questions to ask

Talk with the children about the sorts of animal noises they have made. Ask them if the sounds were high or low, soft or loud? Do they think animals talk to each other? What do they talk about?

For younger children

Can the children make up two things for the farmer to do, help them to describe these to you. Match the animal sounds to pictures of animals.

For older children

Discuss the range of sounds an animal can make, for example, a dog growls, barks, yaps and yelps. What do these different noises tell you?

Use a mirror to show how our mouths change shape to make different sounds. Help the children to remember how their mouth, lips, tongue and teeth feel for different letters.

Follow-up activities

- Visit a farm or take a walk around your setting listening to all the sounds you can hear.
- Play a game where you have to remember, sequence and build up a list, such as; 'Old Macdonald called for his sheep and his cows...' and so on.
- Make a display showing pictures of various animals and detachable cards with the words 'baa, moo...' and so on.

TEDDY AT THE SEASIDE

Learning objective
To draw on the children's own experiences to stimulate talk and make up stories.

Group size
Three to four children.

What you need

A copy of the story *The Teddy Bears Who Went to the Seaside*, Susanna Gretz (A & C Black). Small plastic bears, sand tray, pieces of wood, boats, cloth, twigs, a deep dish, a toy Jeep/open car, card, felt-tipped pens and scissors.

Setting up

Set up the sand tray as a seaside scene; tip the sand tray up at one end or use the deep dish to make part of it as the sea. Include some shells, seaweed or plastic ferns. Use the card to make some mini signposts saying 'To the beach'.

What to do

Read *The Teddy Bears Who Went to the Seaside* to the children.

Talk to the children about the seaside. If they have been then ask them to talk about it. Help them to describe their experiences by asking them to complete some simple sentences, using personal pronouns, such as: I liked ...; I saw...; I played with... and so on. Try and encourage them to use some simple 'time' vocabulary, such as: last week, yesterday and last year. Help them to use simple verbs, past and present.

Next, let the children, in small groups, explore the resources in the sand tray. Encourage them to retell the story in their own words, using the props to help them. They can then go on to use the resources to tell stories in the sand about their own seaside experiences.

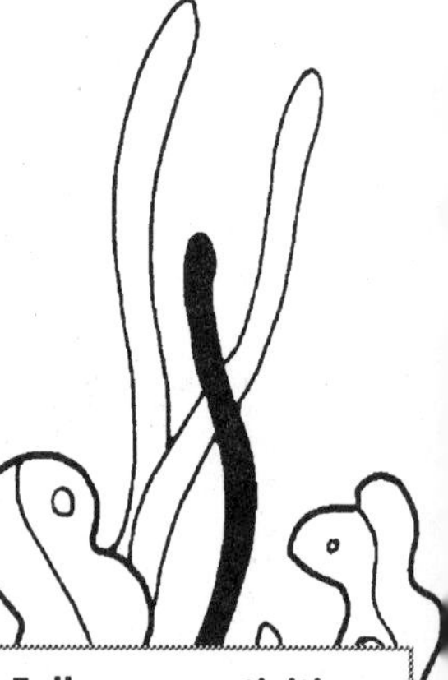

Follow-up activities
- Use the photocopiable sheet on page 59 to show what the teddy will pack in his suitcase when he goes away on holiday.
- Make a list together of all the things you might need to take on holiday.

Questions to ask

Ask the children questions to help them recall and sequence the events in the story: Where did the bears go first? How did they get there? What did they do when they got there?

For younger children

Use some sentences from the story for them to repeat and act out in the sand tray. They will enjoy playing with the bears in the sand, encourage them to talk about their play and ask them about other things that they do at the seaside. Can they show you in the sand tray?

For older children

After the children have used the resources in the sand to retell the story, ask them to make a picture-story to tell the story of a trip to the seaside that they have been on or would like to go on. Their story must have at least three pictures to show a beginning, middle and end.

MAGIC JEWELS

Learning objective
To encourage oral story-telling.
Group size
Individual, pairs or small group.

What you need

A collection of shiny jewels. Cassette recorder and microphone, A3 drawing paper, coloured pencils, scissors.

Setting up

Bury some jewels in the sand tray. Prepare some books. Fold a sheet of A3 into four, open it out, and draw a large jewel on the bottom right hand section. Cut round two sides of the shape and fold the sheet back into four. You will now have a lift-up flap, shaped like a jewel in the centre page.

What to do

Show the children some of the shiny jewels. Tell them that they are magic listening jewels that you can find in the sand in the desert. Explain that some are hidden in the sand tray. To hear the secrets of a jewel you need to uncover it from the sand and put it to your ear and imagine what it is telling you.

Ask the children to uncover the jewels (ensure that each child finds one). Join in and pretend to listen to a jewel, telling the children what its secret is. Help hesitant children by giving them some key clues such as: Humpty Dumpty met Little Bo Peep, what did he tell her? Teddy went for a picnic on the beach, what did he see?

Finally, use the books you have made and encourage the children to draw their secret under the jewel.

Questions to ask

What can you hear in the jewel? Do all the jewels tell the same story. How has the story got into the jewel?

For younger children

Tell them that the jewel has magic powers – it can grant your wishes. Have a discussion with the children, find out what they would like to ask it and what they would wish for.

For older children

In their jewel books, the children could draw more detailed pictures and if ready to do so attempt to write some words to describe what they 'heard'. Encourage the older children to share their books and their ideas with the whole group.

Follow-up activities
- Play listening games such as Pass the whisper.
- Make a play telephone by joining two containers with a length of string.
- Make a desert environment in the sand, making cactuses with Plasticine and using toy camels.

SAND JOURNEY

Learning objective
To understand and follow the sequence of a story.

Group size
Whole group, follow up in small groups.

What you need

Ideally use the book *We're Going on a Bear Hunt* by Michael Rosen (Walker Books), but any story about a journey would also work. Objects for the sand tray to make the scenes of the journey: grass, swamp, pond, cave, a gate and a place for 'home'. Play people.

Setting up

Let the children help you set up the sand tray to represent the scene.

What to do

Tell the rhyme and encourage participation, actions and movement. Emphasise the use of prepositions: *through* the long grass, *over* the swamp.

Questions to ask

What do we need to put in the sand tray? How would you feel if you met a bear? What would you do? Have you ever felt scared? What is it like?

For younger children

Work with them in the sand tray, repeating and emphasising the words of the rhyme as they re-enact the story. Ask them to tell you about their own journey to school. What are the important points, the bits they like, the places they don't like.

For older children

Ask them to change the scenery and make up a new journey. Encourage them to use descriptive language to say where they are going – creeping through the deep dark forest, running down the long lane.

Follow-up activities
- Make an obstacle course outdoors for the children to follow.
- Play the 'Throw a feeling' game using photocopiable page 60. Attach the photocopied sheet to a baseboard. Children take turns to throw a dice, each number corresponds with a 'feeling'. The child must then talk about that emotion.
- Look at other journey stories such as *Rosie's Walk*, Pat Hutchins (Picture Puffin).

RHYMING GAMES

Learning objective
To begin to associate sounds with patterns in rhymes.

Group size
Small groups of two to six children.

What you need
The story *Each Peach Pear Plum,* Janet and Allan Ahlberg (Picture Puffin), sand tray. A collection of objects that each have a rhyming partner, such as: a hat and a cat; a pen and a hen; a fox and a box; a sock and a clock.

Setting up
Hide the rhyming objects in the sand tray.

What to do
Read the story to the group. The pages have an 'I-Spy' theme, connecting the pictures with a rhyming couplet. Let the children enjoy looking at the pages and trying to find the hidden images.

Practise making rhymes using the children and objects in your room, such as: Claire sits on her chair; Jenny found a penny; James is good at games. Help them by starting a rhyme and letting them supply the final word – We drove far in my little ... .

Let a small group of the children go to the sand tray and discover the two sets of hidden objects. Help them to lay out the objects, matching them up in pairs, such as hat and cat.

Questions to ask
What is that called? What other words sound like that? Can you find another one?

For younger children
Let them hide objects for each other to find. Can they remember what they have hidden? Can they give a clue without saying exactly what it is?

For older children
Can the children think of some more words to go with the pairs of objects found in the sand tray. Collect as many different words to rhyme as they can, for example, car/far/bar/jar. Draw pictures of these words and place them in a small zigzag rhyming book.

Follow-up activities
- Use picture and object matching games.
- Have a Treasure Box, decorate the outside with patterns, buttons, sequins. Put a wide collection of objects inside for the children to explore.
- Play spot-the-odd-one-out. Start with two words that rhyme and one that is different.

SAND POEM

Learning objective
To work together to produce a group poem.

Group size
Five to eight children.

What you need

Cassette recorder, stimulus pictures of sand and sea. Large sheets of paper and a felt-tipped pen.

Setting up

Create an intimate atmosphere, either by placing the sand tray at ground level for the children to sit around, or by placing chairs around the tray. Fill the sand tray with fine, dry sand. Cut some of the paper into smaller pieces to use as word labels.

What to do

Sit the children around the sand tray and show them the pictures. Let the children play with the sand, running it through their fingers as you talk together about the sand and the pictures.

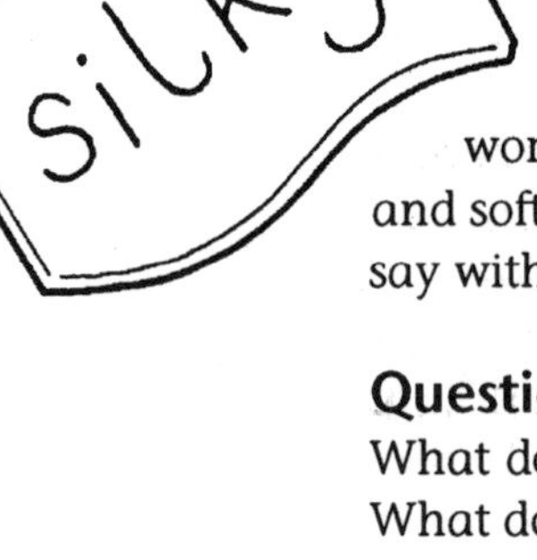

Choose five or six of their words and write them onto the paper labels, showing the children what you are doing and saying the words together. When they have finished describing the sand, move the word labels around saying each word they have given you. Decide with the children the sequence of words they like best. For example: silky, smooth, tickles, runny and soft! Try to make the sequence into a rhythm for the children to say with you.

Questions to ask

What does the sand feel like? How does it move? What colour is it? What does it make you think of? What can you do with it?

For younger children

Younger children will enjoy hearing the sounds of different words in a sequence. They may like to concentrate on repeating two or three words, such as, itchy tickle! Write these down.

For older children

Write their word poem onto a large sheet of paper and read it to them. Ask the older children to record their poem onto a cassette for the rest of the group to listen to. Some children may be able to introduce a tune and sing their poem.

Follow-up activities
- Build up a collection of rhymes, riddles and nonsense poems to share with the children.
- Make finger puppets to go with the children's favourite rhymes.
- When children are familiar with a poem, start it off and let them finish it. Alternatively, say the poem but make an obvious mistake. The children will enjoy telling you where you went wrong!

MATHEMATICS

This chapter explores ways of using sand to help develop young children's mathematical skills. Some activities concentrate on the use of pattern, whilst others develop mathematical vocabulary, counting skills and early mathematical concepts such as one-to-one correspondence.

IMPRESSIONS

Learning objective
To recognise and create patterns and use mathematical language.

Group size
Groups of up to four children.

What you need
Damp sand in a large tray or in small trays, a collection of objects that when used to print in the sand will create some interesting patterns such as combs, fir cones, cotton reels, beads and unifix cubes.

Setting up
Check that the sand is slightly damp and then rake it ready. Smooth the surface and try printing with some of the objects first.

What to do
Initially let the children select an object from the collection. Print with them and then look carefully at the pattern. Let them try to repeat their pattern. Allow them plenty of practise before moving on to the next stage.

Now make a pattern for them to copy. At all times use appropriate mathematical language and encourage this in the children. Can the children describe what they have done? Can they tell someone else how to copy their pattern? Each time a new pattern is required, smooth over the sand to begin again.

Questions to ask
What shape is this? What kind of pattern is here? Can you see anything else that may make a pattern like it? Can you make this set of patterns? What comes next?

For younger children
You may prefer to use a selection of moulds with younger children. Their control and grip may not be adequate to deal with smaller objects. Restrict the number of combinations in the patterns you use to two or three.

For older children
Older children can cope with longer and more complicated pattern sequences, and you could also introduce other attributes such as big/small to extend the activity.

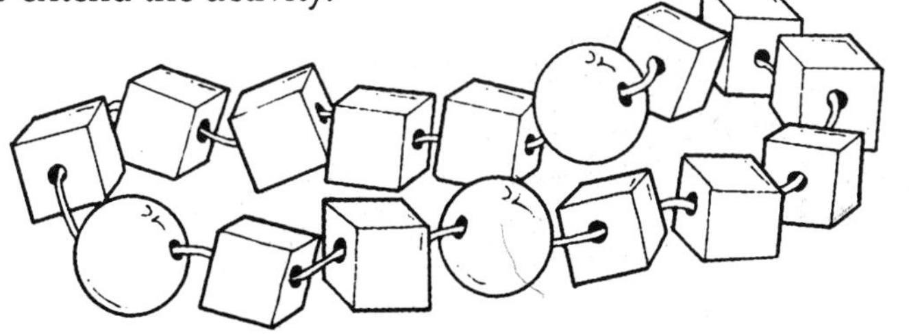

Follow-up activities
- Bead and other threading games.
- Make up some pattern cards by printing some objects with paint onto card. The children can copy these and try their own.
- Look for some patterns in the natural environment.

FILL THAT SHAPE

Learning objective
To recognise and name basic mathematical shapes.

Group size
Group of four to six children.

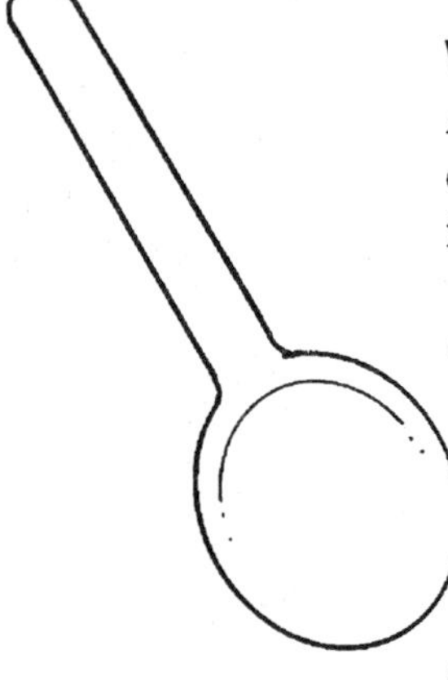

What you need

Damp sand in a tray, a selection of plastic containers that can be filled (it is possible to buy sets of these), spades or spoons.

Setting up

Make the sand slightly damp, not saturated or it will stick inside the containers (test them out first to be sure of positive results). Put out the containers/shapes and give the children a spade or spoon each.

What to do

Ask the children to choose a container and fill it up. Take the opportunity to use language that is linked to understanding capacity, for example, full/half full.

Ask the children to carefully tip out their shape and ask them to describe it. Help them to understand terms such as sides, curves and edges. See if the child knows the mathematical name for the shape. If they do not know, tell them its name and reinforce this by asking the child to find you another 'square' shape from around the room or in the tray. Repeat the process using the other shapes.

Questions to ask

What is the name of the shape? What does the shape feel like? Which is your favourite shape? What do you like about it? What shape are wheels? What shape is a window?

For younger children

Younger children need to have plenty of experiences of using and playing with shapes. Give them opportunities to feel and explore shapes in a number of cross-curricular activities, such as using construction kits, modelling with reclaimed materials and using plastic shapes to print with. They will gain much satisfaction from filling and emptying the containers. Capitalise on this by encouraging them to understand and use the relevant vocabulary.

For older children

Once the children are confident with the name and use of the appropriate mathematical names for shapes, encourage them to recognise shapes in the environment and refine their descriptive shape vocabulary. Ask them to create some repeating patterns using the shapes.

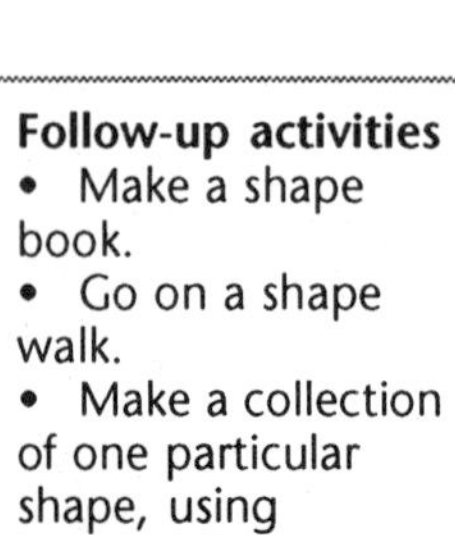

Follow-up activities
- Make a shape book.
- Go on a shape walk.
- Make a collection of one particular shape, using comparative vocabulary to describe them.

SAFARI WORLD

Learning objective
To use an imaginary setting to count, classify and sort objects.

Group size
Small groups of children.

What you need
A collection of wild animals found in Africa (educational suppliers and some toy shops sell whole sets which include the appropriate trees and also jeeps). Pictures of animals from magazines and holiday brochures.

Setting up
Ensure the sand is dry and fine. Put out all the animals, vegetation and any other suitable props. Put the pictures up on the wall or close to the sand tray.

What to do
To begin with, look carefully at the animals with the group. Can any of the children tell you the names of some of the animals? Allow them to play freely with the animals, intervening and prompting them to choose groups of animals based on certain criteria. Use the children's observations to lead naturally into the activity.

Begin to structure the activity by directing the children to find a group of animals that are for example, 'stripy' or 'brown'. Once the children are able to find a set of animals that meet your criteria, see if they can make up a set of animals themselves. Are they able to explain their choice to the group?

Now mix up all the sets and challenge the children to create a different set, based on another set of attributes. Encourage the children to describe their sets to you and each other, throughout the activity.

Questions to ask
What are the names of these animals? Do they live in a cold/hot place? Can you find the animals that are the same?

For younger children
Allow the younger children to look closely at the animals, they may want to make the noise that the animal makes!

Help the younger child to sort the animals using one criteria only, keeping it to simple attributes such as colour.

For older children
Older children may be able to cope with more sophisticated ways of sorting the animals. Encourage them to use a wider range of attributes when making their sets. For example, can they find a set of animals that run fast, or have four legs? Some children may be able to sort using two or more criteria at the same time, for example making a set of animals that are stripy and have four legs.

Follow-up activities
- Make a simple hole in the sand and pour in water to create a water hole for the animals.
- In the imaginative play area put rucksacks, hats, shorts, binoculars and cameras and pretend to go on safari.
- Pretend to be different animals using masks.

DINOSAUR WORLD

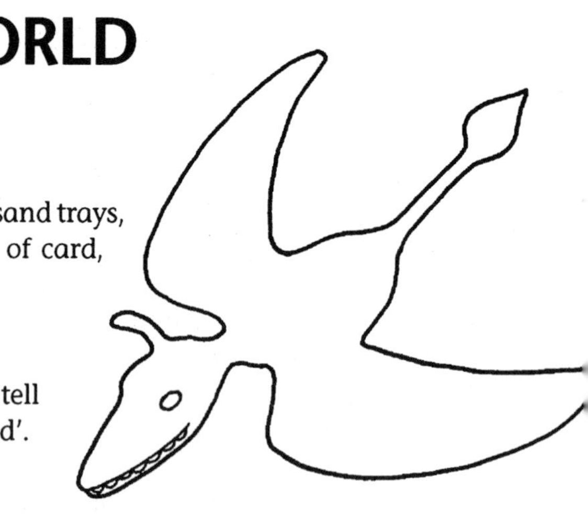

Learning objective
To be able to make comparisons. To sort, count and classify using everyday objects.

Group size
Small group of four to six children.

What you need

A collection of plastic dinosaurs, large or small sand trays, twigs, leaves, pebbles or stones, small pieces of card, felt-tipped pens.

Setting up

Start placing the objects in the sand tray and tell the children you are making a 'dinosaur world'.

What to do

Label areas of your dinosaur world at the children's suggestion, such as 'a dinosaur cave' or 'a swamp'. Give each child a specific area and encourage them to 'become' that dinosaur. Let them enjoy playing with the dinosaurs.

After ten minutes of free play ask the children to sort the dinosaurs to one common property. Are they the same shape or colour? Find a name for each set. Once they are sorted make a place for them in the sand for them to live together. Children will differ in their ability to classify the dinosaurs. Some children will know that some dinosaurs are plant-eaters and others are meat-eaters, for example.

Look at the dinosaurs again. Can you sort them in a different way? Are there any that could go into two sets? Sort the sticks and stones to put around each set. Ask the children to make a space for each dinosaur to have as his home to develop their skills of one-to-one correspondence.

Questions to ask

Which dinosaur do you like best? Why? Where do you think dinosaurs live? Can you see any dinosaurs of the same family? Are there any dinosaurs alive today?

For younger children

Let them enjoy playing with the dinosaurs. Ask if they can arrange the dinosaurs in a long line and with the biggest dinosaur at the front. Vary the activity by changing the attribute of the leader – smallest, tallest or longest.

For older children

Long ago people used to count their animals by putting down a pebble for each one. Can the children count how many dinosaurs are in the sand using this method? How would you know if one is missing?

Follow-up activities

- Use the photocopiable sheet on page 61, 'Match the dinosaurs' to find pairs.
- Make a map of your dinosaur world using collage materials to represent the different areas.
- Read the story *Long Neck and Thunder Foot* by Helen Piers (Picture Puffin).

MAKE THAT PATTERN

Learning objective
To recognise and repeat sequences of pattern made in damp sand.

Group size
This is best done in individual trays.

What you need
A collection of different sized combs, slightly damp sand.

Setting up
Ensure that the sand is damp and that the collection of combs are laid out and ready.

What to do
Demonstrate how a comb makes a pattern when it is pulled through sand. Look at the comb and look at the pattern. Encourage the children to spot the similarities and differences between the comb and the pattern it creates. Allow the children to explore with all the different combs.

Use two of the combs to make a pattern but do not let them see which you have used. Ask the children to try and find the comb and carry on the pattern. When they are confident with this try using three patterns for the children to copy and continue.

Questions to ask
Can you describe this pattern? What do you think comes next in the pattern? Can you make a pattern for me to copy?

For younger children
Pulling the combs through the damp sand will be a good tactile experience for the younger children. Provide a different set of objects in order for them to repeat this skill. Provide some natural objects for them to make patterns with.

For older children
Children who have had plenty of experience of pattern making and following may be able to follow increasingly more complicated and 'erratic' patterns.

Follow-up activities
- Printing and following patterns, threading and following patterns.
- Make some rubbing cards by sticking material onto card for the children to rub over with crayons.

FIVE CURRANT BUNS

Learning objective
To use a familiar number rhyme to develop an awareness of subtraction.

Group size
Group of five children.

What you need
Pebbles for the buns, five circular moulds, damp sand.

Setting up
Prepare the sand. Make it slightly damp. Test to see if the moulds work with the dampness of the sand. Get the pebbles and mix them in with the sand.

What to do
Show the children firstly how to make a pretend bun. Mix up the sand and pebbles and make a 'currant bun'.

After some experimental play ask the children to make one of their own. There should now be five in a row ready to start the song:

'Five currant buns in a baker's shop, round and smooth with sugar on the top.
Along came (insert a child's name) with a penny one day.
Bought a currant bun and took it right away.'

At this point they can squash their currant bun.

Go through the rhyme counting down between each verse and asking questions to make sure the children understand.

Questions to ask
How many are there? One is gone away, how many are there now? Can you check for me? Who has not got a currant bun now?

For younger children
It may be helpful to use some plastic numbers with the younger children. Put them below each currant bun and point and count in sequence slowly and carefully. As each bun is taken away, take away the biggest number to ensure that the 'countdown' makes sense. Keep asking the children how many are left, showing them how to use the numbers to help them.

For older children
Use the correct mathematical language with older children and encourage them to tell you the number story at each stage of the rhyme. For example, 'Five buns take away one bun makes four buns'. Increase the numbers to eight or ten buns for more able children.

Follow-up activities
- Bury objects in the sand for the children to find as another way of practically demonstrating the subtraction process.
- Make a baker's shop in the home corner with a till and money.
- Make some real currant buns and let the children weigh and put in the ingredients.

MOVE IT!

Learning objective
To compare different weights and use mathematical language to describe them.

Group size
A group of four children.

What you need

A collection of identical containers with lids or sealed with paper and adhesive tape to hide the objects inside. A collection of materials such as paper-clips, feathers, stones and string.

Setting up

Fill the containers up before the children arrive and code them so that you remember what the contents are! Make sure that the sand is clear and rake it making two pathways through it.

What to do

Explain to the children that inside the containers are things that need to be moved across the sand tray. Suggest using string to do it. Question them about the weight of the container as they do it, encouraging the use of comparative vocabulary such as 'heavier' and 'lighter'. You may like to encourage them to relate the activity to their own personal experiences and start to name things that they think are heavy or light.

Ask them to decide which container was the heaviest and which was the lightest. Can they place them in order from lightest to heaviest. Later, open them up to show them and weigh them if you can. In doing this activity you are exploring a number of ways to weigh and classify objects.

Questions to ask

Is this easy to get across? Do you think it is heavy or light? What do you think is inside the container? Is it heavier or lighter than the last one?

For younger children

Limit the number of containers to just a few for younger children. Make sure the containers are quite large and easy to pull. Encourage them to make a simple distinction between light and heavy. Talk about other things which are light and heavy with them.

For older children

The older children may use more containers and after feeling the containers could try and predict whether it will be easy or hard to pull across the sand. Do they have any other suggestions for ways to transport the containers across the sand? Ask them to sort another group of objects by weight.

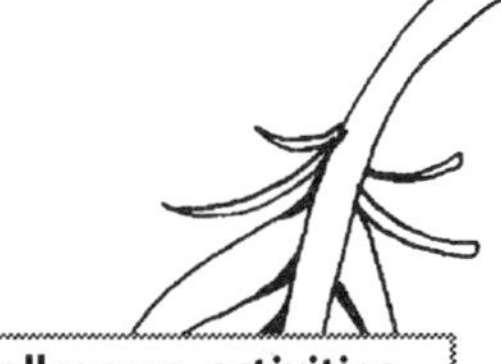

Follow-up activities
- Have a table with some 'heavy' and 'light' things on.
- Set up a shop that sells by weight.
- Find out who has the heaviest lunch box or bag.

MAKE THAT NUMBER

Learning objective
To recognise the way that numbers are written and formed, to practise counting and understand conservation of number.

Group size
A group of four or individuals.

What you need
A set of plastic numbers, dry/slightly damp sand. Large, clear examples of numbers to look at, a collection of objects that can be used in the sand (such as, five toy cars or two trains).

Setting up
Rake over the sand and make it smooth and even on the surface. Get the numbers ready and if possible stick another set of numbers to a nearby wall. Put them in order from left to right.

What to do
This activity will require a close and sensitive approach as the children develop the skills needed to write numbers. Using sand as a material is very supportive as any mistakes that occur can quickly be rubbed out and children can have many attempts.

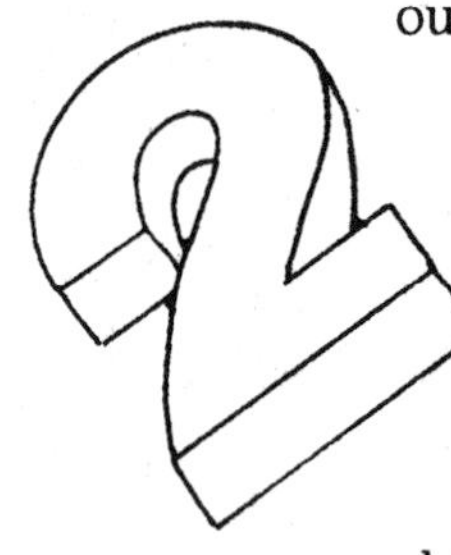

Begin by demonstrating how to form a number using your finger in the sand. Ask the children to try to reproduce it. Always begin at the top of the number. Once the number has been written show the equivalent number of physical objects alongside. Work through the numbers from one to five at first and later five to ten.

Create a display that corresponds to this activity so that the children can practise their skills using other materials when the sand tray is not in use.

Questions to ask
What is this number? How do you make it? Where do you start? How many cars do I put in the sand with this number? If I put them in a row/group how many are there?

For younger children
Limit the numbers used to five with younger children. They may need extra help with difficult numbers such as three and five. To give them confidence in the early stages, help them to use the plastic numbers to trace over with their fingers, giving them the opportunity to experience the way the numbers feel.

For older children
Older children can work upwards to ten repeating numbers that they find difficult to form. Observe them closely, ensuring that they are forming them correctly. Using number rhymes will make the sessions more interesting, try to use those that involve counting up and not down, to avoid confusion.

Follow-up activities
- Make numbers in other materials – in the air, with paint, dough and Plasticine.
- Make a shop with objects that need to be bought by number.
- Make large numbers on the floor with masking tape and ask children to walk along the numbers in the correct direction to the way they are formed.

PERSONAL AND SOCIAL DEVELOPMENT

In this chapter the eight activities focus on ways to develop the children's personal and social skills. Topics covered by these activities include caring for living creatures, working collaboratively to make 'pizzas' and learning about other cultures through patterns and materials.

TAKE CARE TURTLES

Learning objective
To understand the need to respect and care for living creatures.

Group size
Up to four children around a large sand tray.

What you need
Several toy turtles and babies/eggs (available from educational suppliers/toy shops), twigs, pebbles, large sand tray.

Setting up
The twigs and pebbles are to create a simple beach/ island environment. The turtles will have some eggs showing but some need to be buried.

What to do
Establish that these creatures are turtles and how they need care when they are handled or found. Explain that they need a safe and quiet home. They may hide their babies/eggs so that they do not get stolen.

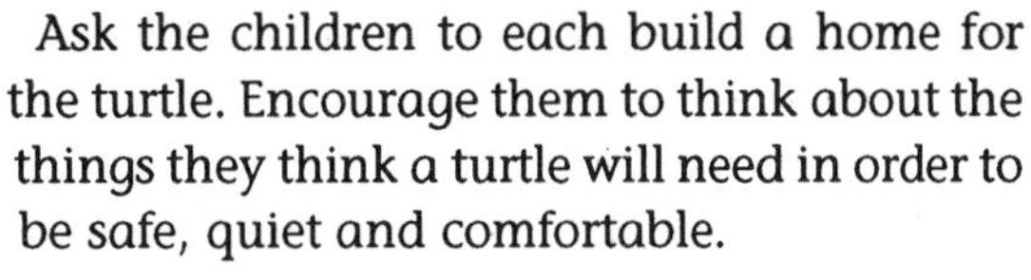

Ask the children to each build a home for the turtle. Encourage them to think about the things they think a turtle will need in order to be safe, quiet and comfortable.

Questions to ask
How do mothers feel when they have a new baby that is frightened? What kind of home would a turtle like and why? What do you think the adult turtles eat? What do the babies eat?

For younger children
Younger children may find it difficult to empathise with the turtles and will benefit from exploring the setting in the sand tray, hiding the eggs in different places. Try to make sure that they understand that they must handle the eggs and turtles carefully so as not to harm them. By answering your questions they will begin to consider what the turtles need in order to survive.

For older children
Share some non-fiction books about turtles with the older children, to give them some more information to use when they are building a home for the turtle. They will enjoy the problem-solving task of building a home.

Follow-up activities
- Make a large turtle from reclaimed materials and some eggs and babies as part of a display.
- Practise moving like a turtle, crawling and digging holes, burying eggs, pretending to swim in the sea.

UNDERGROUND OVERGROUND

Learning objective
To treat the environment with care and concern, to understand how to make things grow and care for them.

Group size
Individuals/pairs or small groups.

What you need
A collection of seeds (large if possible). Some vegetables that have tops on, for example carrots, leeks and beetroots. Plastic watering cans, spades, rakes, deep sand trays, pictures of vegetables, old seed packets.

Setting up
The sand needs to be quite deep and slightly damp. Push some of the vegetables in with tops showing. (Many children will have never seen vegetables presented like this.) Put the garden tools and seeds on a table nearby. Display pictures of vegetables and old seed packets nearby.

What to do
Invite the children to look in the sand to see what is 'growing'. Ask them to pull out one of the vegetables and name it if they can. Then allow the children to investigate the seeds. Ask the children some questions to find out what they know about how things grow, and what is needed to make things grow.

Allow them to replant the vegetables if they wish or plant the seeds and water them. Remind the children to hold the vegetables and seeds carefully. (CARE! Ensure that the children do not try to eat the seeds or put them in their ears or nose.)

Questions to ask
How do things grow? Do you grow? What do living things need? What happens when you plant a seed? Who cares for us? Who do you care for?

For younger children
The main focus for younger children is likely to be the planting and pulling out of the vegetables. Demonstrate how gentle you have to be and how important it is that the hole is deep enough, using this as an opportunity to talk and observe how they behave.

For older children
Older children may enjoy planting some of the seeds. Help the children to record the date that they planted the seeds and make some notes regarding the conditions that they were planted in. Encourage the children to tend the seeds and allow them the personal responsibility for caring for them.

Follow-up activities
- Talk to the children about kindness and care to animals.
- Make some vegetable soup.
- Use the vegetables for printing with paint.

HOUSES

Learning objective
To develop an understanding of the need to take care and pride in their work.

Group size
Up to ten children for the story, small groups for the activity.

What you need

A simple version of 'The man who built his house upon the sand' (Matthew 7 v24-27). The song 'The wise man and the foolish man' in *Okki-Tokki-Unga,* (A&C Black). The sand tray, water in a jug, watering can, rocks, twigs, plastic building blocks, yoghurt pots.

Setting up

Have damp sand, rocks and twigs in the tray. Pile the sand up at either side so that you can make a river bed, then pour in a little water.

What to do

Explain to the children that some stories have special meanings hidden in them. Tell the story in simple terms.

Invite the children to build houses in the sand tray. Remind them that the man who built his house on the rocks took great care to build a strong house. Use the plastic blocks for this. The house by the river was built by a lazy man who built quickly. Make this house out of damp sand, using the yoghurt pot as a mould.

After they have placed the houses let the children create the storm. Pour water from the jugs and the watering can into the river bed. Ask the children to observe and describe what happens.

Finish by singing the song together, using some simple actions.

Questions to ask

Have you ever seen a house being built? Are all houses built in the same way? Why would the house on the sand get washed away?

For younger children

Use the song with the children. Develop a range of simple actions and encourage them to join in at appropriate times. Allow them some play in the sand building different types of houses.

For older children

Let the children build their houses and decide where will be the best place to put them. Extend the discussion to go beyond the face-value of the story. Some of the children may be able to understand the principle behind the story, others may come up with quite original ideas and give you an idea of how they are thinking.

Follow-up activities
- If you have an outdoor sand pit make a den or put a tent in it.
- Try different types of houses in the sand tray.
- Look at other parables and stories from different cultures and religions.

PIZZA GALORE!

Learning objective
To work collaboratively as part of a group.

Group size
Pairs or small groups. (Other children join in as customers.)

What you need
Paper plates, a selection of materials to represent the pizza toppings: sand, salt, different varieties of coloured pasta, coloured foam pieces. Containers for the toppings, a large cardboard box, colouring materials, drawing paper, pictures/adverts for pizzas, boxes for take aways, chef's hats and aprons (optional).

Setting up
Make a label 'Pizza Galore' to go above the sand tray. Decorate the setting with the pizza pictures and items you have collected. Show the different varieties for the customers. Use the large cardboard box as the pizza oven.

What to do
This activity requires the children to work as a team to deliver pizzas to the rest of the group. Within the group the children should have designated roles: one to take the order; one to make the pizza base (damp sand on a plate); one to place the toppings; one to put it in the oven and hand the pizza to the customer.

Play alongside the children, showing them how to pass the plate to each other, pressing in different toppings and saying what they are putting on, such as cheese, ham or sausage.

The other children in the group can come and order the pizza they want, describing it carefully.

Questions to ask
What are pizzas? Have they ever eaten a pizza? What is their favourite topping?

For younger children
Let them role-play choosing whether to be customers or cooks. Encourage them to make polite requests, using please, thank you and may I have?

For older children
Let them design a special pizza, deciding what to put on it and what to call it. Allow them to be responsible for putting the pretend ingredients in the sand tray.

Follow-up activities
- Cook mini pizzas for snack time.
- Design a take-away box, decorating it with appropriate pictures.
- Set up a café in the play area.

SAND PATTERNS

Learning objective
To learn about different cultural events.

Group size
Individual, pairs or small groups.

What you need
Coloured sand, PVA adhesive, pencils, painting materials, paper and card, shallow trays, fabrics, saris and pictures showing paterns from a variety of ethnic and cultural sources: India, Africa, Thailand and China for example.

Setting up
Display the patterns. Prepare the individual trays with a fine layer of sand.

What to do
Talk about the rich and varied patterns. Some of the patterns may be abstract while others represent animals and plants. Find out what the children can see in the designs. Make a sample pattern on card, for example the Mango pattern is a popular design from India. Simplify the design, clearly showing the lines and detail. Make the design large enough for the children to trace over it with their fingers.

Explain that in India at certain times they decorate the paths and the entrance to their house with sand patterns. It is also an Asian custom to paint patterns on their hands and soles of their feet.

Questions to ask
Can you think of special things to do? Discuss celebrations they have experienced–cultural celebrations, birthdays, weddings. Why do you think people make these sand patterns? How do they colour the sand?

For younger children
Show how to draw in the fine shallow sand. Let the children practise drawing with their fingers and other materials. Encourage them to decorate their designs with some oddments, such as sequins, feathers and ribbons. Take one of the sample patterns and ask the children to copy it.

For older children
Ask the children to draw a design on thin card. Carefully go over the lines with PVA adhesive and then sprinkle coloured sand on top. Wait for it to set and then shake off any excess sand. Ask them to embellish their pattern as they wish. Notice their attention to detail.

Follow-up activities
- Make stencils from thin card. Trace a design onto the card and cut it out. Use thick paint and a short stubby brush.
- Find out about different customs and festivals such as Chinese New Year and Diwali.
- Use photocopiable page 64 to make Diwali patterns.
- Look at other cultural decorations such as face painting and face masks.

CHICKEN AND EGG

Learning objective
To understand that young animals need care and protection.

Group size
A group of four children.

What you need
Sand tray, natural materials such as sand, clay, mud, a little straw, grass, wood shavings, egg box, hard-boiled or blown eggs (make a pin-hole at each end and blow out the contents), fluffy yellow chicks such as those sold for cake decoration, books, pictures or photos about chicks.

Setting up
Have the natural materials in the sand tray. Keep the eggs in their boxes until you are ready to use them.

What to do
Explain there is no mother hen to take care of her eggs. Ask the children what they need to do to take good care of the eggs. (They need to be turned and kept safe and warm.)

Introduce the word 'fragile' and discuss why eggs are packed in special boxes. Let the children remove the eggs from the box and pretend play with them in the sand using the natural materials to aid their understanding. Stress the need to be careful at all times.

When you feel the time is right, swap the eggs for the fluffy chicks.

Questions to ask
What is an egg? What will come out of the egg? Is it always a chick? What will the baby chicks need? What can you tell from the size and the colour of the egg?

For younger children
Help them to appreciate the need of handling the eggs carefully. Ask the children to find a good place in the sand tray to place their egg.

For older children
Make some eggs using the clay. Once it is dry, paint it white and decorate it carefully. Use any of the materials to make a nest for the eggs they have made.

Follow-up activities
- Visit a farm to see the hens, ducks and geese.
- Explore the many different ways you can cook and eat eggs: boiled, scrambled, poached, fried, hard boiled, omelette.
- Look at ways we care for human babies. Use their own recent experiences.

THE GOOD SAMARITAN

Learning objective
To understand the needs and feelings of the characters in the story of 'The Good Samaritan' through small world play.

Group size
A group of four children.

What you need

A sand tray with sand, some plastic figures, small spades, twigs, pebbles, water.

Setting up

Make the sand damp and make a valley down the centre of the sand tray with hills either side. Use the spade to do this and then make a pathway, add the boulders and twigs to try and create a landscape. Lay down one of the figures as the injured man.

What to do

Begin the story by telling the children that this man has been attacked, he is ill and cannot move. Let the children ask their own questions about it and then tell the story of the three characters who pass by using a simple version of 'The Good Samaritan'.

Ask the children to retell the story using the plastic people. Ask them to take on one of the roles in the story and work as a group to re-enact the tale in the sand tray.

Questions to ask

Why did some of the people not help? What did they do? Have you ever helped anybody? How could you help if you saw a boy or girl who had fallen over?

For younger children

Make sure that the story is simplified enough for the children to understand. These children will find it hard to work in a group. You may like to observe them at free play with the characters, noting how much of the story they are able to recall and incorporate in their imaginative play.

For older children

They may role-play the story easily and add their own touches! Ask them to go on and work with a partner to make up their own story in the sand tray about somebody who needs help.

Follow-up activities
- Set up a 999 telephone where children can role-play.
- Change the home corner into a hospital to encourage some role-play about caring for others.
- Make some get well cards for people they know who are ill.

STEP THE STONES

Learning objective
To practice sharing and turn-taking in a small group.

Group size
A group of at least four children.

What you need

A collection of boulders or pebbles (these can be numbered if required), a large dice, toy cars, counters, pictures of the children.

Setting up

Put the boulders or pebbles in a line or trail in the sand tray. Get the dice ready but do not decide who should start.

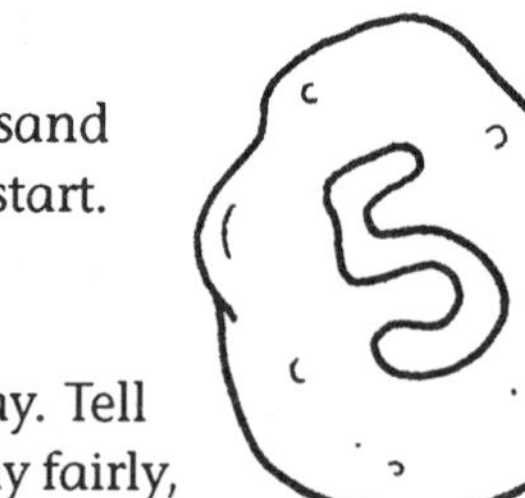

What to do

Position the children, one on each side of the sand tray. Tell them they are playing a game and they will need to play fairly, take turns and share the dice. Ask them what they want as a counter. Tell them they can choose a car, counter or a picture of themselves.

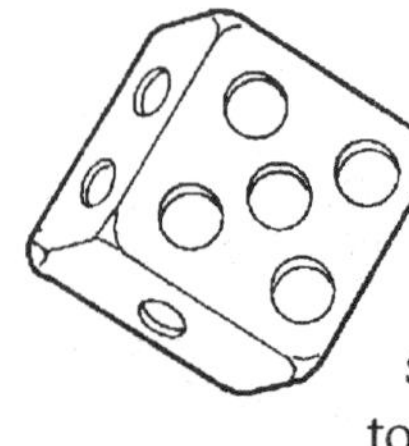

They then need to decide who goes first. How will they decide? The adult may need to intervene at this point in order to get started. Play the game and at the end encourage the children to congratulate the winner and talk about how it is important to be a good loser.

Playing the game: this is a simple, throwing the dice and moving game. They just 'step' from one stone to the next. The start is at the boulder which says one and the end at the boulder which says ten.

Begin at one end of the tray, put the stones in a line. The object is to get to the other side. Use a green spot on the stone for start and a red spot to show it is the end of the game.

Questions to ask

Where do we start? Who goes first and why? What do we have to do to win the game? How do you feel when you lose?

For younger children

Young children will need help and encouragement to take turns and this needs careful monitoring. It may be easier to have the children working in pairs rather than in groups. Make a dice that only has one or two dots on each face for these children to use. Using a reward such as the winner can choose who starts the next game rather than a prize is a good way of helping the children to understand fairness of play.

For older children

Play the best of five games to establish a winner. They may wish to introduce things like 'miss a go' or 'move on two' if they play a lot of games. Try to have some pens and paper or sticky labels and help them to write out some of the new instructions for the game onto the pebbles themselves.

Follow-up activities

- Ask the children to make up a new game in the sand for them to play.
- Talk about real races, such as, the boat race, or the Olympic Games.
- Tell stories about races such as, 'The hare and the tortoise' (Aesop's Fables).

KNOWLEDGE AND UNDERSTANDING OF THE WORLD

This chapter provides activities to increase the children's understanding and general knowledge of the world they live in.

Help the children to understand aspects of the natural world, living things and their habitats through activities such as creating miniature gardens in 'Gardener's world', and homes for plastic snakes in 'Snakes and stones'.

THE BUILDING SITE

Learning objective
To become aware of forces and to explore pushing and pulling objects. To ask questions and solve problems.

Group size
Small group, working in pairs.

What you need
A collection of plastic diggers and lorries, LEGO bricks or DUPLO, wood, string, materials such as blocks, small stones, gravel and coarse sand. A sand tray/baby bath/large plastic sheet to hold the sand.

Setting up
Make the sand sufficiently wet so that the lorries and diggers become stuck, (to resemble a very wet building site). Have the pieces of wood and other resources available.

What to do
Explain that it has been raining all night and when the workers come to the building site, where they are building some new houses, they become stuck in the wet ground. What will they do?

Allow some time for discussion, asking the children some open-ended questions.

Observe the children as they try to solve the problem. Allow the children some time to try to push, play and experiment with the materials. Intervene when necessary, prompting the children with questions and leading them on to new ideas. Provide the range of resources and allow the children to experiment with them.

Questions to ask
Why do you think the lorries are stuck? Have you ever been stuck? What did you do? What materials would be good for a path?

For younger children
Younger children will find it more difficult to work in pairs. Encourage them to feel the difference between pushing and pulling an object. Help them to describe the wet and the dry sand. Ask them to build with the wet sand and dry sand. What does it feel like?

For older children
Ask the children to find ways to move things and then decide which works best, a push or a pull? Fill up the lorries with sand or materials. Do they move more easily when they are full or when they are empty?

Follow-up activities
- Use the photocopiable sheet on page 62 to trace the route of the lorry back to the house, practising pencil control.
- Use dry salt instead, then wet salt. Is there a difference?
- Try to find out how builders lift heavy objects.

GARDENING FUN!

Learning objective
To explore and recognise features of the natural world, looking closely at their similarities and differences.

Group size
Small groups of children.

What you need

Different pips, seeds, cereals and nuts (a pack of muesli or a packet of bird food), gravel, small stones, pots with holes in the base for the plants, saucers, small gardening tools, a watering can, sand mixed with compost, sawdust, shredded paper, tops from vegetables such as carrots, parsnips, radishes and turnips, pictures of gardens, such as Monet's garden or a Japanese garden.

Setting up

The children need to plant the seeds in advance and wait for them to grow. Attach one of the seeds to a card and keep it with the relevant pot. To avoid disappointment make sure you have some fast growing varieties such as mustard and cress, beansprouts, alfalfa. Oats, radish and lettuce also grow quite quickly. Fill the sand tray with the mixture of sand and compost. Collect the plants and the tools.

What to do

Look at the pictures of gardens with the children and discuss them. Work alongside the children as they arrange the plants they have grown in a tray to make a miniature garden. You may prefer to keep the plants in their pots or transfer them to the sand/soil in the tray.

As you do this talk with the children about how to care for plants and the conditions they need.

Put the vegetable tops onto saucers of water and fix in the tray. Water the plants as needed.

(CARE! Make sure the children wash their hands after handling soil and ensure that they do not try to eat the seeds or place them in their ears or nose.)

Questions to ask

Will plants grow in anything? What do plants need in order to grow? Can you tell by the look of the seed what will grow? Where shall we keep the garden?

For younger children

Examine some of the seeds and talk about their shapes and colours. Encourage them to use words such as soft, sticky, striped or furry. Let the children choose which of the seeds they wish to plant and which growing medium – compost, sand, sawdust or shredded paper. Help them to plant their seeds carefully in a pot. They may like to decorate their pots with brightly coloured paints.

For older children

Ask the children to create features in their garden: pathways, pools, a bridge, a fence or a gate. Can they draw a picture to show where all the things go in their garden?

Follow-up activities
- Make cut-and-paste gardens using the photocopiable sheet on page 63.
- Look at different vegetables and talk about which part we eat.
- Compare the different leaves of flowers and plants. Look at shapes, colours and patterns. Print the leaves onto paper or fabric.

ROCK AND ROLL

Learning objective
To look closely at natural materials.

Group size
Four to six children.

What you need

A selection of gravel, pebbles, rocks and stones, sand, a brick/block and a plank, assorted pieces of wood.

Setting up

Put some of the rocks and sand in the tray. Keep the rest of the resources close by.

What to do

Ask the children to examine the different rocks and talk about them. Encourage them to look at the colours and textures. Hold them and compare their weights saying which ones are heavy.

Ask the children to sort the stones into piles, how will they decide to sort them? Find some stones that they think will roll and put them into a pile.

Make a hill in the sand and let the children think of different ways to roll the stones. Show them how to make a ramp with the brick and the plank.

Questions to ask

How can you sort the stones? Can you find a better way to roll the stones? Does the size of the brick make a difference to the way the stones roll? How can you find out?

For younger children

Ask the children to put the big stones into one pile and the little stones into another pile. Make a circle with the little stones. Make faces and figures with the stones in the sand. Make the ramp for the children to roll their stones on.

For older children

Use a hand lens to look at the surface of the stones. Rub two stones together and try to make sand. (This works best with red or yellow sandstone.) Does it work with all the stones? Show them some sandpaper and demonstrate how you can use it to smooth the wood. Let them try.

Follow-up activities

- Find some smooth pebbles and paint pictures on them.
- Tell the traditional story *Stone Soup* (about an old man who tricks a woman into making him a vegetable stew by telling her he has a magic stone).
- Use the stones outdoors for construction and building play.

SNAKES AND STONES

Learning objective
To use miniature world play to learn about living things and their habitats.
Group size
Groups of four, or individuals.

What you need
Dry sand, some plastic snakes, rocks, pebbles, stones, twigs, leaves, books and pictures about snakes.

Setting up
Involve the children in helping you set up the environment by grouping the stones and pebbles, sticking the twigs and leaves into the dry sand and hiding the snakes.

What to do
Talk to the children about creatures' homes, what can they tell you about them? Introduce the idea of snakes' homes and talk about them. Try to have any pictures/books about snakes close at hand for the children to refer to if necessary.

Ask them to find or build a home for the snake. They do not need any spades or tools. They should use their hands and fingers. Try and encourage the children to show where the snakes may go and let them tunnel and be as imaginative as possible.

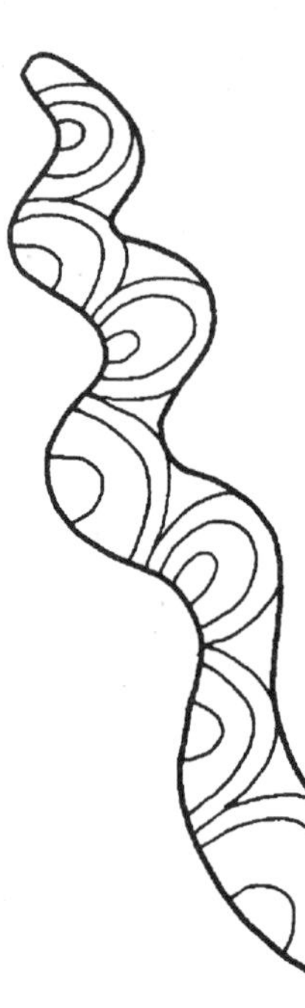

Questions to ask
How does a snake move? Where does it go to sleep? Can you make its house using these objects? Do they live underground or overground? What do they eat?

For younger children
Digging, holding and hiding are the main natural activities for the younger child. Encourage them to hold the snakes and play with them, as opposed to being frightened. If they are frightened let them use mini nets or tongs to help them overcome their fear.

For older children
Talk about hibernation with the children and help them to think carefully about how to prepare a home for the snake. Encourage them to use reference books to give them ideas. Ask them to draw the snakes as an extension of the activity.

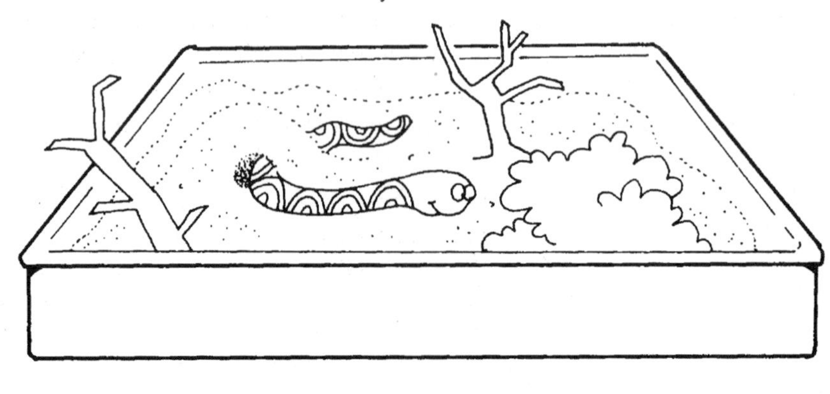

Follow-up activities
- Moving like a snake, wiggling and twisting about.
- Making some 'snake music' and as it is played the snake comes out.
- Making snakes by cutting paper into coils.

PIRATE'S TREASURE

Learning objective
To recognise some objects and use them as starting points for discussion. To observe similarities and differences. To record their findings.

Group size
Individuals, pairs or small groups.

What you need
A collection of small boxes, a small plastic treasure chest, collection of interesting objects such as an old key, a stone, a ring, a shiny jewel. Plastic pirates, paper and pencils.

Setting up
In the sand tray hide some objects under the sand and leave some slightly showing. Put the treasure chest in with its lid open and the two pirates close to it. This will set the scene.

What to do
Take the children over to the sand tray and make up a story about the pirates, saying that they have hidden/lost their treasure and they do not have a map to find it. Explain that they need some children to help them find their lost things!

Select one of the objects yourself. Show the children how to look at it very carefully and ask questions about it. What do you think it is? Who might have used it once? Draw the object and let the children watch you do this. Now it is their turn.

When the children find anything they must talk about it either to you or to a friend. Have available some pencils and paper so that they can record their findings. You may wish to record any comments they have made on the back of their paper to remind you of their approach to the activity.

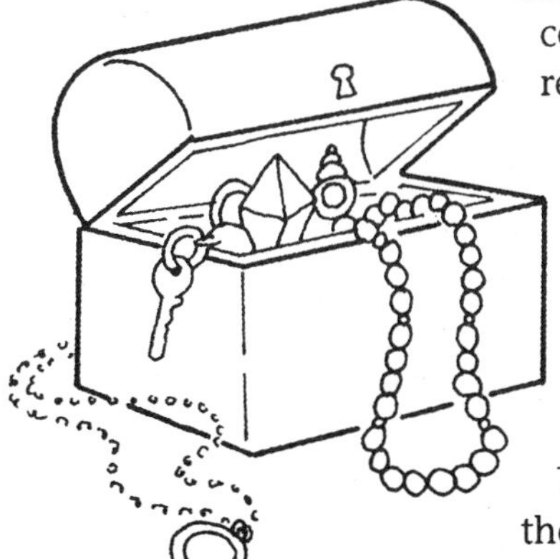

Questions to ask
Where did you find this treasure? How do you think it got there? What is it made of? Is it old or new? Who does it belong to?

For younger children
These children will want to dig and delve and quickly find the treasure. Allow them to find the whole collection and put them on one piece of paper. Talk to the children about the things they found. They could then hide the objects for the next group.

For older children
Older children may need to have some more intriguing objects to stretch their thinking. An unknown object may lead to a problem-solving exercise. They could make a map to show where the treasure was discovered or make a new map and bury the treasure again for the next group.

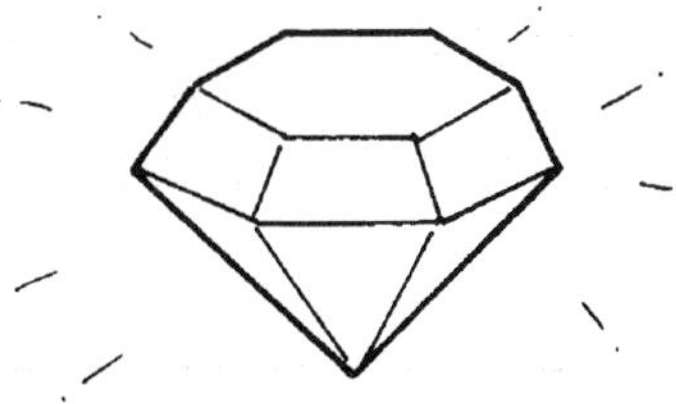

Follow-up activities
- Have some draw string bags/exciting boxes with mystery objects in.
- Ask children to collect and make their own treasure bag/box.

INSECT WORLD

Learning objective
Using miniature world play to understand insects and their habitats.

Group size
Up to four children.

What you need
Sand or soil, cocoa pods (as an alternative), plastic mini-beast set, twigs, small logs, leaves, stones.

Setting up
With the children's help, make a miniature 'garden world' ready for the insects. Lay some logs or twigs down, stand some twigs up like small trees. Arrange the stones in groups, scatter some leaves on the surface.

What to do
Put the insects in a jar or box and introduce the activity in an exciting way by saying to the group 'Let's have a look at what I have here.' Very carefully open the container and gently pick up the insect as if it was a real one. Let the children look and they will soon realise it is made of plastic. Talk about the insect you are holding. Ask them what they know about it? Give each child an insect. Ask them to think about where it lives and what kind of home they could make for it. Let them investigate their insects and think how they will create a 'home' for it. They can use all of the things in the sand tray. Encourage them to talk about what they are doing. When they have finished with their insect they may choose another one to play with or they may swap with the others.

Questions to ask
What is this insect's name? Have you seen a real insect like this? Tell me about it. Where might this insect live? What could it eat? Why have you built the insect's home like this? What do the insects need in order to survive?

For younger children
Restrict your selection of insects to more familiar insects such as bees, ladybirds and flies. Allow the children to work with a friend if they wish. Show them some pictures of the insects to stimulate discussion.

Older children
Older children will quickly become absorbed in this activity. Allow them to select any other resources, such as reclaimed materials that they think they will need for their insect homes. Encourage them to do some research, using some children's reference books, to find out about the insects and their habitats.

Follow-up activities
- Making dens for themselves and pretending to be insects themselves.
- Observe real insects through drawing and talking.
- Read a collection of insect stories,such as *The Bad-Tempered Ladybird,* Eric Carle (Penguin).

NEIGHBOURHOOD WATCH

Learning objective
To enable the children to acquire a sense of location and become more aware of their immediate environment.

Group size
Four to six children with an adult.

What you need
Sand tray, small play blocks, scrap materials; twigs, pebbles suitable for shaping and reshaping their designs.

Setting up
Have the sand tray and scrap materials ready.

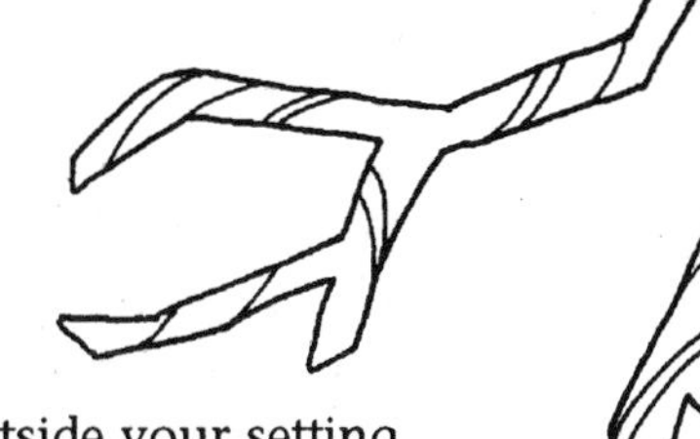

What to do
Take the group for a walk in the environment outside your setting. Encourage the children to look up, down and all around them. Young children will be more aware of the things that they notice at their height level, make sure that you get down to their level to talk about their experiences with them.

Talk with the children about the things that they find interesting.

When you get back to your setting help the children to make a representation of the walk in the sand tray. You will need to remind them of the things that they noticed, help them to create a design incorporating them.

Questions to ask
Is there a road in your design? Do you have a road outside your house? Do you have to cross a road to get here? What do you like best/least about where you live?

For younger children
Encourage younger children to talk about what they see. Try and help them to recall three things that they noticed, as they passed along the route.

For older children
Talk to the children about where they live and encourage them to make a three-dimensional map representing their house and garden in the sand tray.

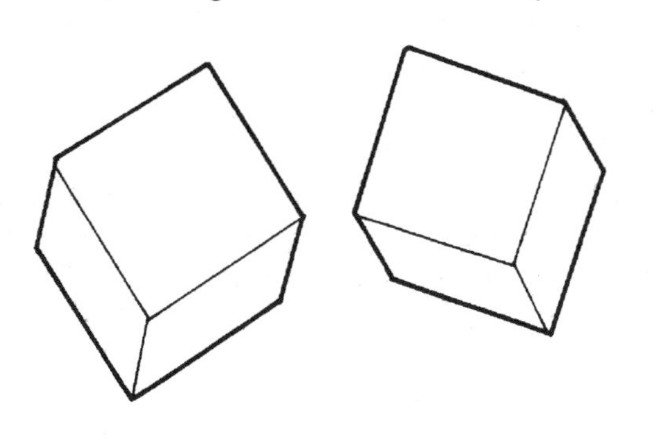

Follow-up activities
- Make large paper footsteps to follow a route around the room or outside.
- Ask the children to paint their routes to the setting, describing what they pass on the way.
- Make a simple board game. Draw a curvy road, marking it off in squares. Illustrate with pictures of the things around your setting. Take turns to throw a dice and move along the route. Who can get to the play area first?

BIRTHDAY TEA

Learning objective
To develop awareness of past and present events in their lives.

Group size
Four to six children.

What you need

Sand tray, cake-cases, pastry cutters and various sand play tools, twigs and other materials to make pretend candles and decorations.

Setting up

Prepare the sand tray with damp sand and have the tools readily available.

What you do

Ask the children to tell you how they came here this morning/afternoon. Help them to think of three things that they did before they arrived. Can they put them in the right order? Talk about the routine and pattern of the day, they will be beginning to understand that certain things happen after others. Try and use as much 'time' vocabulary as possible.

Talk to the children about their birthdays. Is their birthday soon or have they just had it? Can they remember their last birthday, or a birthday party that they went to recently? What presents did they give/receive?

Ask the children to imagine a birthday party that they have been to. Encourage them to make a birthday cake and some of the things that they ate at a birthday tea in the sand. As they work initiate plenty of discussion using 'time' vocabulary and help them to place events in relation to the present.

Questions to ask

What did you do when you got up this morning? What will you do before you go to bed? How old will you be on your next birthday? How old are you now? What things do you like to eat at a birthday party? What games do you like to play at a party?

For younger children

Ask the younger children to think of three things they do during the day, help them to decide which one comes first and which one comes last. Encourage the children to remember a birthday tea that they have been to, or ask them to decide what they would like to eat at their next birthday.

For older children

Older children will be more aware of how old they are now. Ask them to make cakes with the correct number of candles for their last birthday, their present age and their next birthday.

Follow-up activities

- Take photos of the children and use them at a later date to recall what they were doing and what was happening.
- Bury some old objects in the sand tray for the children to find and talk about. Who did they belong to? What were they once used for?
- Make a display of things the children had when they were babies, such as a feeding bottle, a rattle and some clothes. Talk about why they don't use them anymore.
- Make a set of pictures showing a sequence of events, such as a flower growing or baking a cake. Ask the children to put them in the correct order.

Improve and develop the children's co-ordination and physical skills with the eight activities provided here. Many use sand to encourage hand and wrist development and control, such as, 'Roll the conker' where the children have to manipulate small round objects using controlled actions.

ROLL THE CONKER

Learning objective
To use fine motor skills during a practical activity concentrating on finger and wrist movements.

Group size
Small groups, pairs or individuals.

What you need
A collection of tubes made of plastic or cardboard, conkers or small balls, transparent container, dry sand in a sand tray.

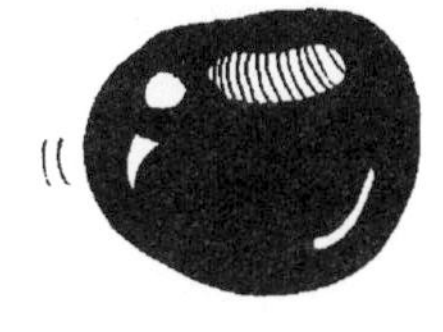

Setting up
Check that the sand is dry and fine as these are the best conditions for this activity. Collect the selection of tubes and put them in the sand tray. Put the conkers or small balls in a transparent container and place in the centre of the tray also.

What to do
Invite the children to choose a tube. Let them hold it, look through it and experiment with it. Ask the children to push the balls or conkers through the sand gently, making tracks and patterns and using different parts of their hands.

Now put the conkers or balls through the tube. Ask the children to rock the tubes back and forward to move the conkers or balls along them.

The children will need to be told to do this slowly and hold the tubes with one hand each side in order to control the direction of the conker or ball. Can they twist their wrists to see if they can spin the conker or ball inside the tube?

Questions to ask
Will the conker take longer to go through this tube than that? Can you keep the conker inside the tube? Can you blow and make the conker or ball move?

For younger children
See through plastic tubes will allow younger children to see and follow the conker or ball as it travels up and down. You will need to demonstrate how to tilt the tube and tip it slowly. Younger children will need plenty of practise at rolling the conkers in the sand using different parts of their hands. This a good physical fine motor exercise. Encourage them to use their fingers and palms, flicking, underhand rolling and manipulating the objects in as many ways as they can.

For older children
Count how long it takes to make the conker travel along, the fastest, the slowest. Fix lots of tubes together to make things more complex, with corners to turn so that their hands and wrists are used with more control.

Follow-up activities
- Repeat this exercise on a large scale using play tunnels outside and large balls.
- Look at how animals who live in tunnels move. Pretend to be them – crawl on your stomach, back, side.

SANDPIES

Learning objective
To gain control of objects and use manipulative skills.

Group size
Individuals, pairs or small groups.

What you need
Large container for the sand, containers of different shapes and sizes such as: bun tins, egg cups and yoghurt pots, foil food containers, seed trays. Rolling pins, scoops, ladles, spoons, spades. Objects to decorate the pies: buttons, shells, stones.

Setting up
Start the activity using only the damp sand in the tray and have the containers to hand.

What to do
Initiate the play by saying you are going to make some pretend pies. Ask the children what things they think you will need.

Choose one of the containers and talk through what you are doing. 'I am putting in two spoonfuls of flour (using sand). Now two spoonfuls of sugar (using sand). Mix it well. Press the mixture down, smooth the surface flat and turn over and out. Now decorate with a cherry (a button) on the top.'

Ask the children to help you and make a pie of their own. Can they remember the sequence to follow?

Make sure that the children fill the pots to the top and push the sand down well into the container, compressing it and making it flat. They will be using hand and eye co-ordination as well as small muscles in the finger and thumb. They will be grasping, carrying, lifting and pouring.

Questions to ask
What must you do to make a really good pie? How can you make a big pie? Find the container that made this pie? Can you make a pie to fit onto this saucer/plate?

For younger children
Encourage the children to try and do it alone. Observe how they prepare themselves for the task, collecting the right container and spoons, preparing and making the pie. Help them to follow the sequence you showed them.

For older children
Use verbs to describe their actions as they play: pat, push, pinch, squeeze, punch, stroke, mix the sand. Talk about how the sand feels as they work: rough, cold, soft, fine, smooth, bitty, gritty. Let the children work together to build the biggest pie in the world. Observe how they approach the problem.

Follow-up activities
- Mix flour in with the sand to produce a different texture.
- Introduce containers with different shaped necks. Will they still be able to turn out pies?
- Investigate the best texture for making pies (not too dry, not too wet).

MASHER

Learning objective
To use a variety of tools, using fine motor skills to grip and manipulate them correctly.

Group size
Groups of up to four children.

What you need
A sand tray with wet/dry sand in. A collection of kitchen utensils such as a potato masher, sieve, strainers (these should be a mixture of stainless steel, plastic and wood).

Setting up
Display the collection of utensils so that the children can see the whole range. Rake the sand tray so that the surface is even and unmarked, ready for the children to explore and experiment.

What to do
Ask the children to look at, name and explain what they think these tools are used for. Allow them to press and mark the surface of the sand to observe and experiment with the marks that they make.

Continue by asking them to press down using varying degrees of force. Allow the children to swap and explore each other's utensils, controlling the tools to make and copy each other's patterns. Demonstrate the hold on each tool and show them how to use different forces such as pushing and pulling which will involve using fine motor skills.

Later, play a game: ask them to shut their eyes while you mark the sand. Can they guess which tool did this?

Questions to ask
What is this tool called and what is it for? What happened in the sand? Will another tool do the same? Describe the patterns you have made on the sand.

For younger children
It may be worth using the home corner/play corner utensils with younger children as they may find the adult tools too difficult to manipulate. Limit the number of tools that you introduce initially, to ensure that quality time is spent exploring each tool. Choose a selection of tools that will enable a variety of skills to be developed, such as rolling, pushing and pressing.

For older children
Older children will be able to cope with a wider selection of tools. Encourage them to focus on two or three of those selected and explore the number of ways they can manipulate and use them. Can they count how many different ways?

Follow-up activities
- Use the same tools for cookery; make some mashed-potato and strain some tea-leaves.
- Use the tools to do some paint printing.

TRICKLE TREAT

Learning objective
To develop fine control and gain confidence in handling small tools.

Group size
Individual, pairs or small groups.

What you need

Fine dry sand, sieves, funnels, pipes or tubes.

Setting up

Set up the tray with dry sand. Have the selection of containers to hand.

What to do

Begin by watching the sand as it trickles through an egg timer. Encourage the children to observe it carefully. Ask them to describe the movement of the sand.

Now lift up some sand and let it fall into the tray. Show how when you pour dry sand into the tray it builds into a cone shape. As you pour on more sand the base of the cone enlarges.

Show the children how to clench their fists to make a container for the sand. If they carefully release their little finger they can let the sand trickle out. What does it feel like as it escapes through their fists? Can they stop and start the trickle? Allow the children plenty of time to experiment at making cone-shapes, feeling the sensation of sand in their hands and between their fingertips. Allow them some time to experiment with the rest of the resources.

Questions to ask

What did the sand feel like when it trickled through your hand? What shape is it making in the tray? What will happen if we pour on more sand?

For younger children

Encourage them to plunge their hands into the fine sand, burying them, opening and closing their fists in the sand. Let the sand fall through their fingers. Can they feel the softness and the free flowing sand?

For older children

Ask them to make several cones of different sizes, using their fine control to vary the amount of sand they allow through their hands. Allow the older children to experiment with a sand wheel and some sieves, watching how dry sand behaves as it sprinkles onto their hands.

Follow-up activities

- Put sand onto the surface of a drum or a tin lid and move it around. How does it move? What sounds does it make?
- Use a magnifying glass to see the grains of sand. Are the grains of sand all the same shape, size and colour?

FEEL IT

Learning objective
To handle a variety of natural materials safely and with increasing control.

Group size
Four to six children.

What you need

A variety of natural materials such as: wet and dry sand, rice, flour, sawdust, lentils, pot-pourri, stones, sieves with different meshes, seed trays, shallow dishes, a blindfold.

Setting up

Prepare the sand tray with half wet and half dry sand. Have the selection of other materials ready in pots or dishes. Loosely group them according to size, shape or colour.

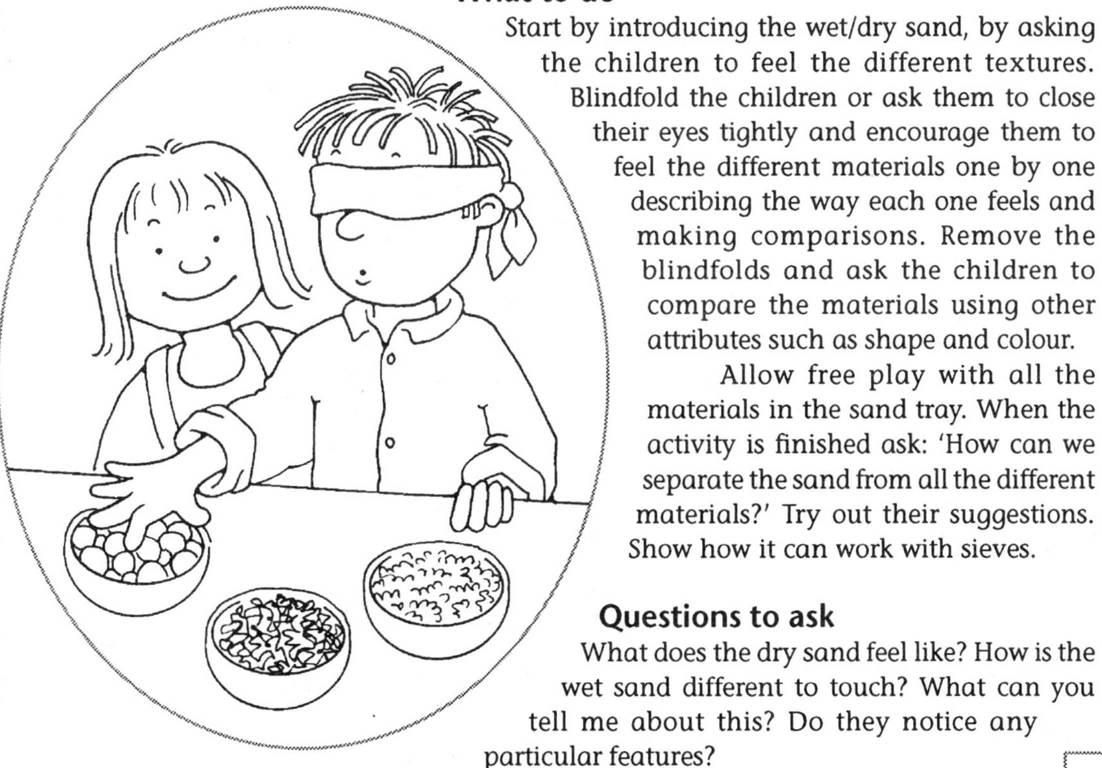

What to do

Start by introducing the wet/dry sand, by asking the children to feel the different textures. Blindfold the children or ask them to close their eyes tightly and encourage them to feel the different materials one by one describing the way each one feels and making comparisons. Remove the blindfolds and ask the children to compare the materials using other attributes such as shape and colour.

Allow free play with all the materials in the sand tray. When the activity is finished ask: 'How can we separate the sand from all the different materials?' Try out their suggestions. Show how it can work with sieves.

Questions to ask

What does the dry sand feel like? How is the wet sand different to touch? What can you tell me about this? Do they notice any particular features?

For younger children

Describing more than one attribute is difficult for young children. Restrict the variety of materials so that they are not confused with too many variables. For instance use flour and rice which are the same colour but different in texture and size. Help them by summing up what they have said.

For older children

Put four materials onto separate trays according to the way they feel to touch. Ask the children to find other materials to put on the tray saying why or how they can belong to the group. They should find a matching attribute – slippery, spiky or soft, for example.

Follow-up activities

- Find out which surfaces produce good rubbings.
- Stick different grades of sandpaper onto a baseboard in the shape of a house. Put matching samples into a bag. Pick one out and say where it belongs – roof, windows or door.

DIG IT

Learning objective
To develop the use of fine motor skills through a practical sand activity using a variety of tools.

Group size
Small groups of four around a sand tray/ pit.

What you need
A variety of plastic sand tools, spoons – wooden and metal, a sand tray with wet or dry sand in, wrapped sweets or toys to find.

Setting up
Hide some treasure under the surface of the sand. It could be toys or wrapped sweets. Then rake or smooth the sand over to show no trace of where the treasure may be. Put all the tools at the side of the tray or pit.

What to do
Explain to the children that there are some objects to find in the sand and they need to dig to find them. Give them the option to select the best tool they can think of to dig with. They may swap their tools during the activity providing that they have negotiated the swap with their peers.

Throughout the activity the children will be experimenting with different types of grip, using their fine control to manipulate the tools accurately.

Questions to ask
Can you tell me where you think the treasure is? How deep will you need to go? What tool will dig the deepest/quickest?

For younger children
It will be necessary to provide short handled tools so they can co-ordinate them with more control avoiding collisions with the other children! You may like to provide spades for the children to begin with, but do encourage them to hold and explore other tools so they experiment with the grip they will need.

For older children
Include a variety of wooden and metal tools so that children have to explore and experiment with the feel and control that different tools will need. Encourage the children to hold and use the tools with a variety of actions. Some will discover this by trial and error and some by imitation of others. Observe how they cope with different tools and techniques.

Follow-up activities
- Help the children to do some planting and digging.
- Set up scenarios like workmen digging up the road in the home corner.
- Organise a treasure hunt in your setting.

HIT AND MISS

Learning objective
To encourage large body movements with hand/eye co-ordination. To develop control of an object.

Group size
Individual, pairs or small group.

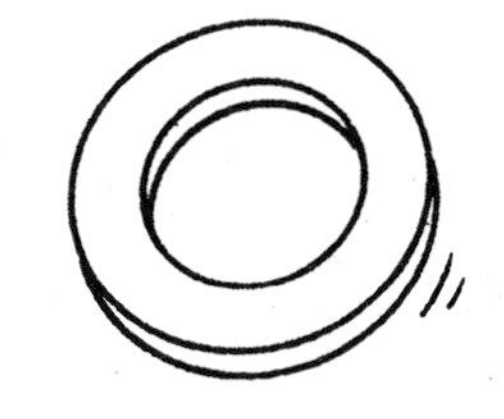

What you need

Sand tray, small cotton cones (factory waste) or plastic bottles. Small hoops, balls or bean bags.

Setting up

Fill the sand tray with damp sand and place it at ground level. Arrange the cones/bottles to stand upright in the tray. Try to have a variety of shapes and sizes. Mark out a standing line (this is a good activity to have outdoors).

What to do

Show the children where they must stand and how to throw their hoop at the targets. Decide if you want them to circle the target or knock it over. As they become adept at the task encourage them to move a little further back. Can the children invent any new rules for the game, or think of another way to play it?

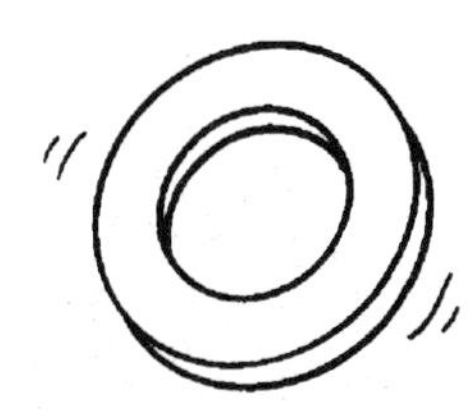

Questions to ask

Which object is the best one to throw? How can we decide who goes first? How can we make it more difficult? Do you know any other throwing games? What happens if you throw the things too hard?

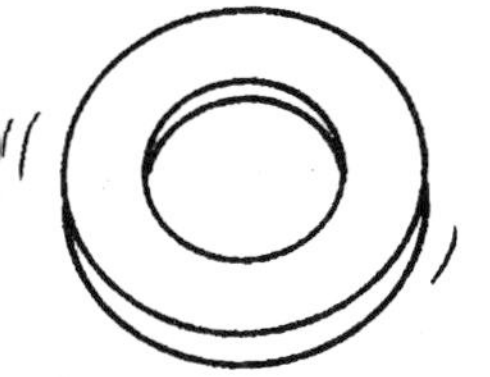

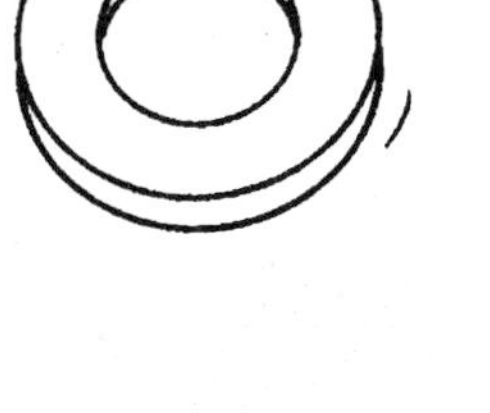

For younger children

Young children may need plenty of practice to hit the objects. Begin by using the empty sand tray as a target. Let them stand quite close to the tray. As the children become more adept, introduce three well spaced out cones.

For older children

Encourage the children to aim at a specific target - choosing the colour, shape or size before they throw. Move the standing line to make longer or shorter throws. Put obstacles among the bottles/ cones.

Follow-up activities

- Have an obstacle course outdoors. Place no more than six objects for the children to run around, space them well out.
- Develop the children's large arm movements and control by asking them to pretend to be helicopters or windmills. Give a signal for starting and stopping.

DIG DEEP

Learning objective
To develop gross motor skills using a variety of equipment to dig in the sand.

Group size
Small groups/pairs/individuals.

What you need
Spades with different length handles, buckets, plastic crabs/creatures. A large floor sand tray.

Setting up
Hide the creatures deep in the sand. Rake the sand over so that the children can't see where the creatures have been hidden.

What to do
Explain to the children that at the seaside there are many creatures who hide deep down in the sand. To find the creatures that are hidden the children will need a bucket to collect them and a spade that will dig deep into the sand.

Let the children select a spade and ask them to dig a very deep hole to find the creatures and put them in the buckets.

Ask the children to count the creatures as they collect them in their buckets. Encourage them to keep looking until all the creatures have been found.

Questions to ask
What kind of creature are we looking for? What does it look like? Why do you think it may be hiding? What do we do when we have found a creature?

For younger children
Younger children will find it difficult to co-ordinate long handled spades. Give them a spade that they can manage and bury the creatures nearer to the surface. Help them to count the creatures.

For older children
Ask older children to work with a partner and take it in turns to hide creatures for each other. Make sure that the person searching hides her eyes! They could give each other 'hot and cold' clues as they dig.

Follow-up activities
- Play a game of hide-and-seek with a group of children.
- Play 'Kim's Game': use a selection of sea creatures and sand tools.
- Make simple maps to show where treasure is hidden.

CREATIVE DEVELOPMENT

The opportunities for using sand to develop the children's creative and imaginative skills are explored in this chapter. Children will experience sculpting sand, exploring textures and creating sand collage pictures. In 'Picnic dance' they will use sand to create musical instruments and as a stimulus for dance and movement.

SAND SCULPTURES

Learning objective
To explore and represent familiar objects in 3-D form.

Group size
Up to six children working individually or in pairs.

What you need
Sand tray filled with sand, containers of various shapes and sizes, moulds, bun tins, pastry cutters, large buttons, shells, rolling pins, sand in salt shakers/sprinklers, sieves with different sized holes and meshes.

Setting up
Make the sand just damp enough to hold shapes. Have the other resources close at hand.

What to do
Tell the children that they are going to try and make pictures in the sand. To begin with, show them how to roll the sand flat and press their hands in to make an imprint. Do the same with the shells. Let them experiment for a while and then show how to shape the sand with their hands and the containers, building up, piling one on top of another. Encourage them to try for themselves.

Ask the children to create specific shapes, such as flat, wide or round shapes. Help them to describe the shapes they are making.

Try introducing the concept of capacity, is the container full, half-full or empty. Is there enough sand to fill the containers?

Questions to ask
Use open-ended questions to encourage them to think about the activity such as: What did the sand do? Why did it break up? How can you make a circle?

For younger children
Show younger children how to use a sand shaker/sprinkler. Help them to make pictures and shapes in the sand by varying how much they sprinkle. Show them how to gather large amounts in a container or mould.

For older children
Challenge them to make a whole scene using the resources to make shapes and sculptures. They should work together as a team using a large tray. Link it to some other work you are doing together.

Encourage them to ask you for things they will need and describe what they are going to do. Watch how they work and interact together.

Follow-up activities
- Use coloured sand to make exciting sculptures. You can buy it or make your own.
- Work with clay/chalk/block salt to model by cutting away the shape rather than building it up.

STICKPICS

Learning objective
To explore different textures.

Group size
Individuals or small group.

What you need

Sand tray, tubs containing a wide variety of materials: seeds, pasta, rice, wood shavings. Spoons and scoops, sieves with different sized meshes, thick paper or card, paper plates, PVA adhesive, crayons, chalk.

Setting up

Put out the tubs containing the different materials. Make the sieves and spoons available. Keep the paper/card, plates and adhesive close to hand.

What to do

Firstly allow the children to explore the different materials. Encourage them to observe the different shapes, textures and colours, mixing them together in the sand tray. (CARE! Ensure that the children do not try to eat any of the materials or put them in their ears or nose).

After they have played with the materials, show how they can make pictures. Draw a simple shape with the chalk and then spread on the adhesive. Stick on a selection of the materials to make a picture.

Questions to ask

Take a selection of the materials and let the children talk about them. Ask them which ones they like to touch, can they describe how they feel? What shapes are they?

For younger children

Younger children will be fascinated with the different materials and will enjoy exploring their textures. Encourage them to sort them and put them into the tubs. Allow them to choose which materials they want to stick. Give them a paper plate and help them to make a small puddle of adhesive in the centre of the plate. Show them how to place their materials on the adhesive.

For older children

Ask the children how they can separate the different materials? If they are not sure show them the sieves. Demonstrate how the different sized mesh allows different objects to fall through. Challenge them to find the most suitable sieves for each different type of material. Allow them some time to explore and experiment.

Follow-up activities

- Make a rubbing of their picture. After sticking the shapes onto card, place a piece of paper on top and rub over with a wax crayon.
- Write their name in adhesive onto a piece of card and sprinkle the materials on top.

MIX AND MOULD

Learning objective
To explore texture, shape and form in natural materials.

Group size
Individuals or small groups.

What you need
A shallow tray, sand and water, a selection of: clay, flour, salt, lentils, pebbles, soil, compost, powder paint. A selection of patty tins, lids, small frying pan, funnels, stirrers, spoons, sticks, a small dustpan and brush.

Setting up
This is a messy activity so ensure the children wear aprons and cover the working area with plastic sheeting or newspaper. Ideally work outdoors. Keep the small dustpan and brush to hand.

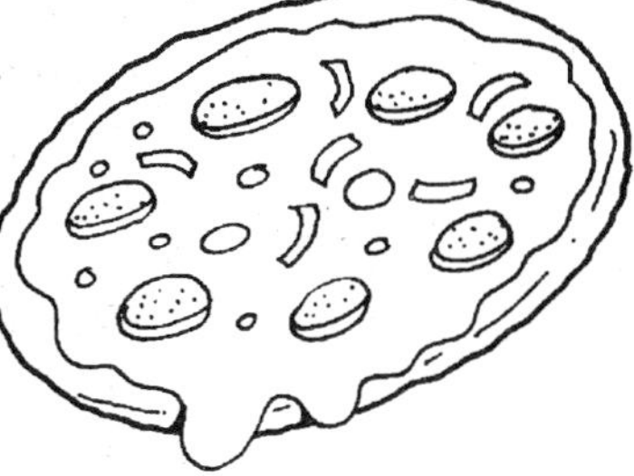

What to do
Encourage the children to mix different materials together. They will be using different skills: mixing, stirring, sifting, pouring, filling, emptying and moulding.

Mix sand and clay to make a gritty medium. Mix clay and flour to make a dough like substance that can be kneaded, rolled or used for modelling. Mix lentils, beans and peas with sand. Add water and stir.

You can now encourage the children to use the moulds to make pretend cakes, tarts, chapattis, pies and pizzas. (CARE! Stress to the children that they must not try to eat any of the materials). The different meshed sieves will separate the materials so that you can reuse them.

Questions to ask
Why do some of the mixes fall down and collapse? Will all the mixes run through the funnel? Which of the materials become sticky when you add water?

For younger children
Young children will enjoy mixing the materials and pretending to cook. Let them experiment and try out different mixtures and ways of shaping them. Are they pinching, patting or squeezing the material? Encourage them to find names for their dishes.

For older children
Let the children see how the materials behave. Can they squeeze it, stretch it, flatten it? Challenge them to make small delicate things with it. Help them to describe the materials, using words such as: rough, slippery, sticky, crumbly and smooth. Ask the children to associate the mixture with things they know. 'When I feel the mixture it makes me think of...'.

Follow-up activities
- Sand, clay and gravel will make bricks. Mix together with a little water, shape into bricks and leave to dry.
- Use sand and adhesive to make Diwali patterns using photocopiable page 64.
- Mix sand into paint to make colourful textured marks and pictures.

DENS

Learning objective
To encourage children to use their imagination and create make believe worlds.

Group size
Individual, pairs or small groups.

What you need
The sand tray filled with one of the following: sand, gravel, lentils, sawdust, compost or salt. Play people, animals, pieces of wood, cardboard, cloth, fixing tape.

Setting up
Start the activity with an empty sand tray. Show the children the different materials and resources.

What to do
Tell the children that they are going to use the sand tray to make a play area. Discuss some ideas with the children, it should be connected to the work that you are doing in your setting and with the children's interests and experiences. You may link it to a theme such as the farmyard – 'Make a place for the animals to be safe and warm'; to their play – 'Make a garden for your dolls'; or it could be fanciful – a shelter on a desert island or a pirate's den. Start the activity with them, asking them questions and helping them to select their materials and resources. Let them spend time selecting and choosing what they need, trying things out, changing and adapting.

Once the children become involved in the activity, fade into the background and use the opportunity for some observation and assessment.

Questions to ask
What will you need? How are you going to...? Will all your people fit in there?

For younger children
Give younger children some more specific directions, such as – 'The dolls want a tea party in the garden', or, 'The rabbits need a place to sleep'.

For older children
Older children should be able to plan their area with more care and forethought. Encourage them to perfect the fine details of their area: What will the pirates eat and drink? Where can they hide their boat?

Follow-up activities
- Use the children's ideas to re-design your role-play area.
- Turn their play into story-making by writing down their ideas.
- Take 'den making' outside and make large scale shelters.

THE PICNIC DANCE

Learning objective
To develop children's imagination through music, dance and story.

Group size
The whole group.

What you need

The Bear Dance by Chris Riddell (Little Mammoth). Different types of sand, yoghurt pots, adhesive, small stones, cassette recorder, some dance music. Dressing up clothes including a head-dress for Jack Frost and a furry hat for the bear. A picnic set and a small table.

Setting up

Fill the yoghurt pots with different types and quantities of sand and small stones. Join them end-to-end with adhesive to form shakers. Arrange the role-play area so that there is room for children to dance. Place the dressing up clothes, sand shakers and cassette recorder within reach. Set up the picnic area to one side.

What to do

Read the *Bear Dance* and talk about it with the children, helping them to identify with the little girl and the bear. Discuss going on a picnic with a friend. Talk about how the little girl felt when the cold and frosty Jack Frost turned up to spoil the warmth of the picnic site.

Explain to the children that you are all going to tell the story, by dancing to the music and pretending to be the characters. Demonstrate some dance steps to stimulate the children's imagination. Act out a small piece of the story at a time, trying out the different moves. The children can also take turns to play the sand shakers in time to the music.

Questions to ask

What did their character do in the story? Use descriptive language to portray the dance movements such as stomping, stamping, tip-toeing.

For younger children

Use the sand shakers or clapping hands to help them get the idea of the beat. Encourage them to role-play the various characters and make up their own dance sequences.

For older children

Introduce the idea of more formal dance steps and working in partnership. Develop the idea of symmetry and mirror work as they dance with each other.

Follow-up activities
Look at the music and dance from other cultures – Indian, African and Caribbean styles.
- Arrange a visit from a dance group.
- Play musical statues, dancing and stopping with the music.

COMB IT!

Learning objective
To use a range of materials and tools to explore texture.

Group size
Small groups.

What you need
Large sized paper that will fit in the bottom of the sand tray, adhesive and adhesive sticks, a selection of various sized combs, dry sand.

Setting up
Put the large piece of paper on a table. Help the children to cover the paper with adhesive, place the paper at the bottom of the empty tray and put about a centimetre of sand on top. Put the combs nearby.

What to do
Show the children how to gently comb the sand across the paper. Explain that they may use any part of the paper, using a variety of patterns. Talk to the children about their ideas, do they have an end-product in mind, or will they just experiment with designs? They will need to co-operate and work as a group, using all their ideas.

When the group are satisfied with their picture help them to lift the paper above the tray to shake the sand off before they move it away. Replace the paper. The children can choose and change the tools they wish to use, improving upon their designs and using their new skills. Replace the sand level for each new group.

Questions to ask
Can you tell me how you made this part of the pattern? What kind of pattern does it make? What part of the picture is yours?

For younger children
Younger children may find it hard to share the space with their peers, observe them carefully to see how they manage to interact.

These children will be at an early stage of exploring shapes and letters, help them to explore making circular movements and lines.

For older children
Older children will be able to use their knowledge of some letters, numbers and shapes. Help them to use their skills of letter and numeral formation to plan their picture. Allow them to help to carry the final picture to the floor and tip the sand off the picture.

Follow-up activities
- Using other natural materials as part of creative work for example, creating collages using materials such as sawdust.
- Use the combs with textured paint to create pictures of waves and the sea.

SAND MUSIC

Learning objective
To develop the children's imagination and help them to express their ideas.

Group size
A group of four children.

What you need

Dry sand, containers with lids on, any materials that will make different sounds, such as: pasta, shells, stones, gravel. A cassette recorder and recorded music.

Setting up

Dry the sand out before you begin the activity. Record pieces of contrasting music. Collect the containers and the materials and present them so that the children can choose and reach them easily.

What to do

Invite the children to join you at the sand tray and ask them to shut their eyes and put their fingers in the sand on the surface. Explain that you will play some music and that you want them to listen carefully. As they listen they should make some patterns in the sand with their fingertips. When the music stops the children must stop and together you can have a look at the patterns that have been made.

Select a piece of contrasting music, smooth over the sand and let the children make some new patterns as they listen. Compare each other's patterns.

Finally, show the children the selection of materials you have gathered and help them to make a musical instrument using the containers. What different sounds have you created?

Questions to ask

Is the music fast or slow? What sounds could we make to go with the music? What kind of sound are you making?

For younger children

Use shorter extracts of music with younger children as their concentration span is less developed. Use music that the children are familiar with. They will need plenty of assistance when making and deciding upon their instruments.

For older children

Encourage the older children to be more imaginative in their choice of instrument to make. Allow them to select any other materials that they think they will need. Encourage the children to work in a group and make up some music of their own.

Follow-up activities
- Listening to music as children paint.
- Taping the children's own musical compositions and listening to it.
- Using sandpaper to make scraping blocks.

SAND PAINTING

Learning objective
To explore texture in two dimensions using a range of materials and tools.

Group size
Small groups or individuals.

What you need

Sheets of ready cut paper, adhesive sticks, paint brushes of various sizes.

Setting up

Smooth the sand level in the tray. Make sure the sand is dry (for the adhesive to work). Gather the brushes, checking they are dry.

What to do

Explain to the children that they are going to use the paintbrushes to make patterns in the sand.

Allow them to experiment and when they are happy with their picture talk about the shapes they have made. Show them how to cover their sheet of paper using the adhesive.

The children then need to carefully and gently lay the paper over the area where they have made their pattern, and then try to 'lift' it off from the surface of the sand. Transport it carefully onto the floor area to dry. When they are dry have a discussion about all the different pictures.

Questions to ask

What pattern/picture have you made? What brushes did you choose? Can you tell me how you made your picture?

For younger children

The main emphasis with younger children should be placed on allowing them to be imaginative with dry materials.

You may need to give more help to the younger child when 'lifting off' the print. Help them to experiment with different patterns, using the opportunity to develop pre-writing skills.

For older children

Extend the activity with older children by allowing them to use a number of different objects for mark-making and by introducing the use of coloured paper.

Follow-up activities
- Try some marbling in plastic trays. Help the children to 'lift' their prints out of the tray.
- Using large paint brushes with water to paint outside.
- Using large brushes in an outside sand pit.

PHOTOCOPIABLES

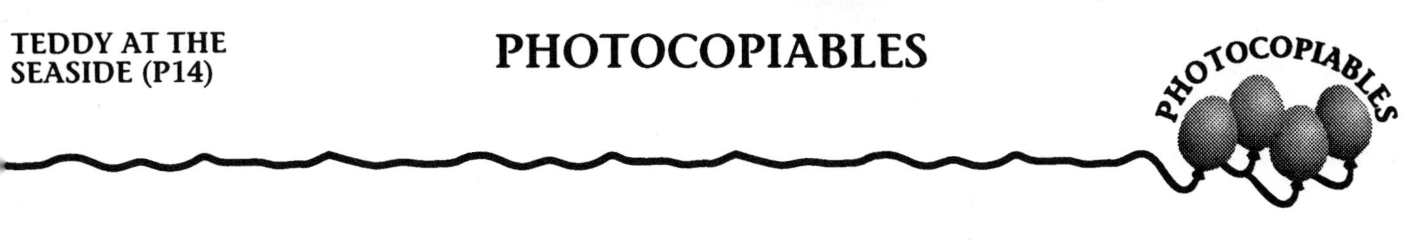

Name ______________________________

Teddy is going on his summer holiday to the seaside. Talk about the picture and draw a line from the suitcase to each thing that Teddy will need to pack.

Name ___________________________

Name ______________________________

Draw a line to match up the dinosaurs to make pairs.
Colour each pair the same colour.

Name ______________________________

Use your pencil to show the lorry the way to the house.

Name ______________________________

Design a garden by cutting and pasting the pictures.
Colour your picture.

Name ________________________________

Paint adhesive onto the shapes.
Sprinkle sand on top. Leave to dry then shake.

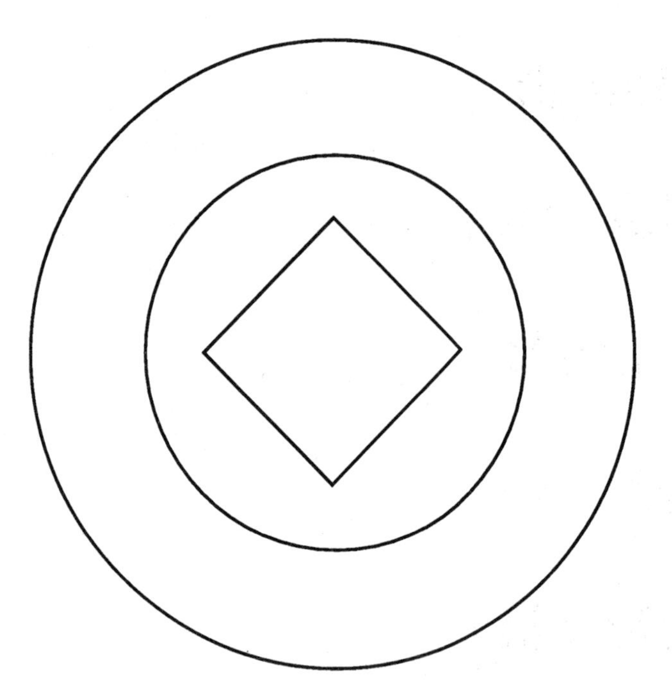

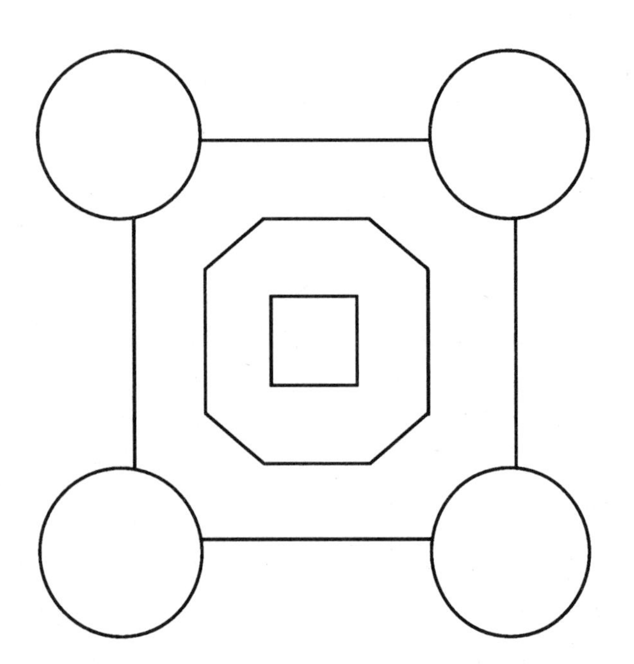